Praise for
TALENT ZONES

"A call to the culture to rethink our methods around developing youth, asking administrators, educators, parents, and coaches to reflect on misguided adult exclusionary tactics around nurturing talent and, in the process, awaken to new, more effective and compassionate ways of developing kids. Lee has clearly 'honed his talent' for summarizing complex information and presenting it in a down-to-earth, relatable way, making this book pragmatic, interesting, and insightful."

—Dr. John O'Brien, psychologist and former Ajax and US Men's National Team player

"Lee Hancock starts with a meditation that flips the script: let's line up ten kids and decide who among them is talented. Feel confident? What if the kid tapped as 'without talent' is your child? What then? What if we rewrote the playbook of selection and opportunity and teaching on behalf of the whole group of ten? This is a profound and important meditation on the thing we call 'talent,' which we assume we understand are able to see."

—Doug Lemov, managing director of Uncommon School and author of
Teach like a Champion and *The Coach's Guide to Teaching*

"*Talent Zones* is a book that could not come at a better time. In our world of competitive overparenting, it is so helpful to have a resource and guide to really get to the root of the definition of talent—where it lies, and how it can be cultivated, nurtured, and built in healthy ways. Hancock encourages readers to focus on the journey and not the destination, to embrace and view failure as an opportunity, and to help kids develop grit. Hancock has deeply researched for readers on a topic we all want to know more about: talent. What it is? How is it identified and sometimes mislabeled? What is the history of its meaning? This is a fascinating read for parents, coaches, educators, or anyone who works with kids."

—Cynthia C. Muchnick, author of six education-related books, co-author of
*The Parent Compass: Navigating Your Teen's Wellness and Academic Journey
in Today's Competitive World,* and parent of Division 1 college athletes

TALENT ZONES

TALENT ZONES

10 Tools to Help Kids Develop Their Talents

Lee Hancock, Ph.D.

Foreword by Tom Byer

free spirit
PUBLISHING®

Library of Congress Cataloging-in-Publication Data
Names: Hancock, Lee (Sports psychologist), author.
Title: Talent zones : 10 tools to help kids develop their talents / Lee Hancock, Ph.D. ; foreword by Tom Byer.
Description: Minneapolis, MN : Free Spirit Publishing, [2022] | Includes bibliographical references and index.
Identifiers: LCCN 2021043834 (print) | LCCN 2021043835 (ebook) | ISBN 9781631986239 (paperback) |
    ISBN 9781631986246 (pdf) | ISBN 9781631986253 (epub)
Subjects: LCSH: Ability in children. | Child development. | BISAC: EDUCATION / Learning Styles | EDUCATION /
    Special Education / Gifted
Classification: LCC BF723.A25 H36 2022 (print) | LCC BF723.A25 (ebook) | DDC 155.4/13—dc23/eng/20211109
LC record available at https://lccn.loc.gov/2021043834
LC ebook record available at https://lccn.loc.gov/2021043835

Free Spirit Publishing does not have control over or assume responsibility for author or third-party websites and their content. At the time of this book's publication, all facts and figures cited within are the most current available. All telephone numbers, addresses, and website URLs are accurate and active; all publications, organizations, websites, and other resources exist as described in this book; and all have been verified as of August 2021. If you find an error or believe that a resource listed here is not as described, please contact Free Spirit Publishing.

Edited by Christine Zuchora-Walske
Cover and interior design by Shannon Pourciau

10 9 8 7 6 5 4 3 2 1
Printed in the United States of America

Free Spirit Publishing Inc.
6325 Sandburg Road, Suite 100
Minneapolis, MN 55427-3674
(612) 338-2068
help4kids@freespirit.com
freespirit.com

FSC
www.fsc.org
MIX
Paper from
responsible sources
FSC® C005010

Dedication

To my sons, Jaden, Gavin, and Owen. You each have unique talents. It has been an amazing journey for your mom and me to watch you pursue your talents over the years. Hopefully you get a chance to read this book and feel we have created Talent Zones for you in your lives. We are so proud of you and can't wait to watch you continue to become amazing young men. Follow your passions and be the best versions of you that you can be. Love you!

Acknowledgments

To my parents: Thank you for giving me the freedom and flexibility to explore my talents in my own time and in my own ways.

To my wife: Thank you for being an understanding and tolerant spouse throughout my career, and of course, during this long and often arduous book writing process. It is true: I do have a fun job, and you have been amazingly supportive of my passions for all the years we have been together.

To my sons: Thank you for being my proving ground for the development of talent. I know I talk a lot about life lessons, being a good person, doing your best, and so on and so forth, but it really is easy when I have such fantastic people to work with every day. Thanks for being awesome kids and making my job—as a parent and talent developer—always exciting and never dull!

To the amazing people at Free Spirit: Thanks! I am in awe of the work you did with my writing. You took a manuscript and made it a book. That manuscript took a long time to write, and I always felt that the ideas in it deserved a set of talented individuals who would make it look and feel like a finished product. I am proud of the work we have done, and I hope I represent your work as well as you have represented mine.

And finally, to John Lincoln: What can I say . . . you laid the groundwork for this book in so many ways. Personally, you challenged me, poked me, prodded me, barked at me, put your arm around me, taught me, and overall treated me as if I could, not as if I couldn't. You never allowed me to make an excuse or blame anyone or anything. You made me a better teacher, coach, parent, and person. You taught me that every single child can learn and should have the opportunity to learn—period. This gift of open eyes, and a passion to pursue education and talent development with that approach, is why this book exists today.

CONTENTS

LIST OF FIGURES

In my three and a half decades as a technical skills developer for young soccer players, I have traveled the world presenting my work in more than thirty countries. One of the great benefits of presenting at conferences is that you get to be around a lot of really smart people. Although you are there so people can learn from you, you are also learning from everyone else. One of my favorite sayings is *If you are the smartest person in the room, you are in the wrong room.*

On one occasion I was invited to Geneva, Switzerland, to present to a group of top professional youth development coaches. It was there that I met Dr. Lee Hancock. We were both presenting at the conference, and a mutual friend had suggested we meet up on the sidelines.

Since meeting Lee in Geneva, I have had many opportunities to talk things over with him—in person, over the telephone, and by text. We are always discussing development, and because of my interest in psychology, I am constantly picking Lee's brain because he's always the smart guy in that particular room. Lee's expertise is multifaceted; he is a teacher, father, researcher, and coach all in one.

Lee traveled in 2019 to Tokyo, where I live, as the sports psychologist for the Canadian women's beach volleyball team. The team had just won the world championship and was playing in a pre-Olympic tournament to get accustomed to Japan. I remember Lee telling me he was writing a book. He said it was taking a huge amount of time because of all the research he was conducting. Well, that book has finally arrived!

Talent Zones puts us in the room with many smart people. Lee has done an outstanding job of seeking them out and dissecting their work, explaining it in detail, and weaving these ideas together into a development model that works—not only in sports, but also in academics and the arts. Many of the experts he quotes are people I look up to, who are all tops in their fields. This book, while small, is actually several books in one. It took me a long time to read because I wrote down so many notes for my own practical use.

After reading this book, I could not help recalling a fourth grader who was always fidgeting in class, clowning around, and distracting other kids. He was labeled as a low achiever. This little boy's teacher once dragged him out of the classroom into the hallway and told him, "You have the brain the size of a pea!" The teacher said he was not smart enough for fifth grade, and his mom agreed to hold him back to repeat a year. Having to repeat a grade is a traumatic experience for any young person. They become ashamed of staying behind while all their classmates advance to the next grade. This boy later tried out for his local Little League baseball team but was once again told he wasn't good enough and played for the Farm League team instead.

But his sister believed in her little brother. She always cheered him on. When he changed from baseball to soccer, she often played soccer with him and encouraged him. She saw his talent and nourished it. He became quite good at soccer and excelled in high school, until he hit another bump. He tried out for the regional all-star team but was told again that he just wasn't good enough. The next high school season he scored the most goals on his high school team and was voted MVP of the league in New York State. This kid went on to play successful collegiate and professional soccer. After his retirement from playing, he helped transform Japan's youth soccer development program. The little boy who'd been told he wouldn't amount to much of anything in his life would also publish four books and five DVDs and win the Golden Boot Award from Adidas International for his contributions to grassroots soccer.

That person is me, Tom Byer. Like many of the people whose stories are told in *Talent Zones*, I was deemed "untalented"—not because I had no talent, but because I needed help finding my passion, growing it into talent, and persevering through rough patches. If it hadn't been for my sister, whose constant encouragement helped me believe in myself, my life would have turned out quite differently.

Through stories and research and his own experience, Dr. Hancock teaches the importance of recognizing the possibilities in all kids and building their self-belief so they can realize their own potential. He offers adults ten Talent Development Zones—practical, evidence-based, developmentally appropriate ways to help kids grow their talent. This is a book that all adults who work with kids—including parents, teachers, and coaches—can benefit from keeping on their nightstand, coffee table, desk, or mobile device, and referring to it as much as possible.

Thank you, Lee, for sharing your wisdom. I will be applying it in both my parenting and my professional work, and I think many other readers will find it just as helpful as I have.

Good luck to everyone involved with developing talent in kids!

Tom Byer

INTRODUCTION

As an educator, sports psychology coach (someone who works with athletes on the mental aspect of their game), and parent, I have worked with talented individuals of all ages and in multiple arenas—from kindergarten classrooms to the Olympics, from high-level young athletes to students in "at-risk" programs. In addition, I have worked with youth talent identifiers and talent developers (teachers, coaches, and leaders) in music, sports, and academic programs. These talent developers have been employed in gifted and talented programs as well as general education classrooms and in elite arts and sports programs as well as grassroots clubs. And in each of these environments, talent—special skill or ability—has emerged.

At the outset, I should clarify that I am focusing on the idea of *talent* and talent development in education, fine arts, and sport as opposed to *giftedness*. The terms *gifted* and *talented* are words used to describe individuals with natural abilities, and in the context of education, these two terms have specific meanings. *Giftedness* in education often refers to natural ability, usually in one or more academic subjects (such as math, writing, or science), that places a child far ahead of their same-age peers. *Talent* in education also refers to natural ability, but usually in nonacademic subjects such as music, dance, or physical activity; talent is often considered innate but also malleable.

Professionals and groups dedicated to the education of gifted and talented children have their own definitions. The National Association for Gifted Children says, "Students with gifts and talents perform—or have the capability to perform—at higher levels compared to others of the same age, experience, and environment in one or more domains" (2021b). The Elementary and Secondary Education Act of 1965 defined gifted and talented students as "Students, children, or youth who give evidence of high achievement capability in areas such as intellectual, creative, artistic, or leadership capacity, or in specific academic fields, and who need services and activities not ordinarily provided by the school in order to fully develop those capabilities." The most recent reauthorization of ESEA, the Every Student Succeeds Act (ESSA) of 2015, retains this definition (Woods 2016). Talent developers in sports would probably agree with each of these definitions, but would define this ability as *talent* and see it as something that is innate yet also built.

> We—as educators, coaches, and other invested adults—have the opportunity and the responsibility to help more kids build, strengthen, and explore their innate talents.

This idea—that talent is innate yet built—is what intrigues me about talent, and it's where I focus my attention. My primary message in this book is that we—as educators, coaches, and other invested adults—have the opportunity and the responsibility to help more kids build, strengthen, and explore their innate talents. And the choice to label kids has profound consequences for them—both positive and negative—early on in school, sports, and the arts.

In sports, education, and fine arts, kids are either placed in or denied access to talent development programs every day based on tests, anecdotal evidence, or other talent markers (or ability to pay for the programs). Adults identify a small percentage of kids as "talented" at an early age and, by omission, unconsciously identify the others as "not talented"—with no proof that kids identified as talented when young will become talented adults, or conversely that kids identified as not talented will not become talented adults. We pour resources into talent development programs while often relegating the unselected to lesser learning environments, where they fend for themselves and either develop their potential or don't.

Why I Wrote This Book

We spend so much time focusing on a small percentage of "talented" kids based on our subjective markers while not providing other potentially talented kids a chance to develop their talents. This book explains why we can and should keep an open mind as it relates to talent in children and how we can give a much greater percentage of children that chance.

Who This Book Is For

This book is for educators, sports coaches, music teachers, fine arts teachers, parents, and really anyone who works with kids in performance settings. As you read the book, I would like you to keep an open mind about talent in kids, including the labeling of talent, the development of talent, and the management—or mismanagement—of talent. For example, I understand that gifted and talented programs in schools, sports, and the fine arts have been around for years, and some are based on sound research. My goal is not to argue against having these programs. Rather, my goals are:

- to examine the idea of talent in relation to sports, education, and the arts, including how we create cutoffs without looking at enough criteria or the right criteria
- to explain how kids who are not labeled as talented can still be talented

About This Book

In this book I describe what I believe talent really should mean when it comes to children. I explain how early talent is currently "found" and mined and how that isn't always the best approach for developing long-term talent. I show how we have been defining talent all wrong, especially in kids. I discuss how being deemed untalented can be either a major opportunity or a catastrophe, depending on one's mindset. I look for ways to redefine the *talent* label as a journey, not a destination. I discuss research-based, practical ideas to help teachers, coaches, and parents create Talent

Development Zones (TDZs) for kids as they journey. You'll notice in this book that I use soccer examples more than once. That's because I've played and coached soccer at a broad range of levels, so I have quite a bit of expertise and experience with this sport.

Part 1: Talent in Kids—What It Is and What It Could Be

The first part of the book provides an in-depth overview of why I think it is critical that we look at talent differently in kids. It explains how the concept of talent has been used over time, the origins of the word *talent,* the research on talent development, and how we can approach talent in children differently—and more constructively.

Chapter 1: Talented or Untalented?

This chapter discusses how children are labeled talented or not as they move through their talent development journey. I describe how kids may be placed on tracks at very young ages based on perceived talent, despite little proof that early talent identification yields consistent results.

Chapter 2: The Concept of Talent as We Use It Today

Here we discuss how adults currently use and misuse the concept of talent with kids. It explains how pop culture, sports, and literature define talent and offers a typical scenario for how talent is developed using the Standard Model of Talent Development (SMTD). I describe the concept of self-fulfilling prophecy and ponder what happens to children who are unselected, or not identified. Finally, I present research showing why our current approach for identifying talent (or not) doesn't work.

Chapter 3: Redefining Talent

Chapter 3 explores the history of the word *talent* backward through the centuries, eventually arriving at the original Greek definition of the word. Then it explains why it's in children's best interests to redefine the concept of talent in kids using this rediscovered definition.

Chapter 4: Reapproaching Talent Development in Kids

This chapter discusses why and how we should reapproach talent development in kids. First I describe what educational psychologist François Gagné's talent development model says about why and how talent develops. Then I discuss the research that shows this model is partly wrong and partly right, because development is nonlinear. We run a high risk of misinvesting in the select few (at best) and completely missing investing in the unidentified many (at worst).

Part 2: Talent Development Zones

Talent Development Zones (TDZs for short) are ten tangible, evidence-based, developmentally appropriate ways to help kids develop their talent. These TDZs transform the concepts and research explored in part 1 into practical strategies adults can use to create environments that help kids develop their own talents.

TDZ1—Embrace Failure as an Opportunity

Here we discuss growth mindset and its parent theory, achievement goal theory. In this section I provide specific examples and practical ideas for how to help build growth mindset in kids using ideas gleaned from the research.

TDZ2—Smash Ceilings

TDZ2 explores the concept of a glass ceiling and relevant research from the US government and classrooms that shows why placing limits on learning isn't a good thing. I explain how we can avoid limiting kids, using specific examples and practical ideas.

TDZ3—Provide Opportunities for Deep, Deliberate Practice

This chapter discusses the importance of deep, deliberate practice and examines the popular idea that ten thousand hours of practice are needed to get good at something. I suggest there's more to the story, based on research by Anders Ericsson and Daniel Coyle. I also provide specific examples and practical ideas for helping kids engage in deep, deliberate practice.

TDZ4—Build Realistic Optimism

I discuss the concept of realistic optimism in this chapter and explain why it is important in developing talent. I offer specific ways to help build realistic optimism in kids using ideas gleaned from the research.

TDZ5—Foster in Kids a Love for Their Endeavors

In TDZ5 I describe self-determination theory and relevant research from Daniel Pink on why it's important to develop a love for what you do. I also discuss ways to help build intrinsic motivation in kids.

TDZ6—Develop and Inspire Creativity

This chapter explains why creativity is important in developing talent. I discuss the creative problem-solving (CPS) theory and provide practical ideas for stimulating creativity in kids.

TDZ7—Build "I Can" Kids

Here we explore self-efficacy and confidence. I describe systematic, practical ways to develop "I can" kids.

TDZ8—Help Kids Manage Pressure

In this chapter, I discuss the different kinds of pressure, or stress. I offer suggestions for how to help kids manage stress emotionally and physically—and make the most of it.

TDZ9—Develop Grit (and Know When to Change Course)

TDZ9 explains the importance of grit, or steadfast courage, determination, and perseverance. I describe the four key components of grit—interest, practice, purpose, and hope. I also discuss how grit may involve a change in direction. I offer specific ideas to help kids build grit and manage change.

TDZ10—Create a Culture of Development

In the final TDZ chapter, I describe what a culture of development is, why it's important, and how it can be built using the power of stories, heuristics, and play. I explain why safety and vulnerability are critical components of this culture. I offer ways to create and develop culture of development with kids.

Conclusion: Enjoy the Journey

The book concludes with a brief overview of what I've set forth throughout the book. It provides a few reminders and ideas to help you enjoy the journey alongside the kids you work with day in and day out.

How to Use This Book

I hope you not only read and enjoy this book, but also learn from it and use it often, in many different ways. I hope you dog-ear a bunch of pages, write in the margins, and mark up the passages that are important to you. I also hope that when I discuss a concept, theory, or researcher who piques your interest, it inspires you to dig deeper. I hope that as you read you'll be eager to try the many actionable points, tips, and suggestions you'll find. And I hope my book generates discussion and spurs you to create even more ideas about talent and strategies to develop it. If you have any feedback or questions, you can interact with me on Twitter @DrLeeHancock or through my website: DrLeeHancock.com.

Lee Hancock

PART 1

Talent in Kids— What It Is and What It Could Be

This portion of the book describes the concept of talent, how it has been used over time, the research on talent and talent development, and how we can approach talent in children differently and more constructively.

CHAPTER 1
TALENTED OR UNTALENTED?

Let's do a little exercise. If I were to line up ten kids and put them through a series of activities designed to show off their abilities in a particular domain, would you be able pick out the ones with talent?

Let me make it easier for you. Let's say that the domain is music, and in the group of ten kids, I put a young version of Aretha Franklin. Or maybe the domain is soccer, and I put a young Lionel Messi in front of you. Or perhaps it is mathematics, and the group of ten kids includes a young Stephen Hawking. Now could you pick out a child with talent? If so, what is the kid doing that demonstrates talent? We can assume from the definitions of the word *talent* in the sidebar that the child is showing some unique abilities, outperforming others, and overall doing things at a higher level compared to the other children in the group.

A Few Definitions of *Talent*

A natural ability to be good at something. (dictionary.cambridge.org)

A special natural ability or aptitude. (dictionary.com)

A special, often athletic, creative, or artistic, aptitude. (merriam-webster.com)

Based on the common definitions and popular notions of talent, I would not argue with you. Those kids—young Aretha, young Lionel, and young Stephen—have some real talent. They have a unique ability—innate or otherwise—that makes them stand out.

But what about the other nine kids? Do they have talent?

Let's look at the group of kids again. Perhaps you have a broader view of talent and you say three more kids in that group also demonstrate unique abilities or potential. So, you identify four kids in your group as having talent.

What about the remaining six kids? Do they have talent?

Let's line up that same group of ten kids, ranking them on a continuum from most talented to less talented to least talented. Could you do that? My guess is, if pressed, you could probably identify one kid you felt had very little talent based on the common definition.

Okay, let's do one more exercise with the same group of ten kids. This time, one of the kids is your child. And this time I am the person deciding how talented each child is. I say, "I have determined that nine of these kids may have talent, but one doesn't have talent." That one is your child.

Your child is untalented.

What would you say about my assessment? How do you feel? What do you think?

You are probably frustrated, bummed out, and irritated. Perhaps you are even comparing your kid to the other nine children and thinking, "I can't believe they're more talented than my child."

You might even tell me I have no idea what I'm talking about. Your child can absolutely be as talented as anyone else in that domain. Your kid *does* have talent; it is just waiting to come out, or your kid needs coaching or teaching. You might tell me that if I had just seen this or that, I would have judged your child differently.

Why Does It Matter?

Why does it matter which kids are identified as talented and which are not? If you are a parent, you probably already know. A child anointed as talented is shown through door number one—the get-attention door. A child thought to have little or no talent is shown through door number two— the sometimes-get-attention door.

Through door number one is a place where talent is developed in the few kids identified as talented. This place offers access to the best teachers, directors, leaders, and coaches. It is a place where lots of people pay attention to a child's development. It's where the best academic programs (such as gifted and talented programs and honors classes), schools, and school systems are found. It's where kids find sports clubs and select teams. It is where children are invited to music conservatories or theater programs. Frequently, door number one leads to more and more "good" doors.

A child anointed as talented is shown through door number one—the get-attention door. A child thought to have little or no talent is shown through door number two—the sometimes-get-attention door.

Through door number two is a place where adults sometimes see kids' abilities and try to help develop them. Or it's a place where children must get after it themselves. This place often has lots of kids in it, and the teacher, leader, director, or coach is just trying to get stuff done. Children may or may not develop their talent here, but that isn't the primary focus. Neither the expectations nor the environment is designed with this goal in mind.

These doors exist in every performance domain where children participate. They lead to consequences, both for the "talented" and the "untalented." When we adults create, open, and shut these doors, labeling kids and showing them through one door or the other, we are setting them on track at an early age to receive all that is behind the chosen door.

Which door is better? Does being identified as talented mean a child will succeed? Does not being identified mean a kid won't succeed?

I think most parents would want their children to be selected as talented because of the reasons I've just described. What if I said that being labeled talented carries some potential problems and that being labeled untalented could begin a beautiful journey on a road less traveled—one that could actually lead to more talent?

In fact, many talented people have been labeled untalented at some point. From Michael Jordan (who famously wasn't selected for his high school basketball team) to Maya Angelou (who as a child was viewed as unintelligent because she didn't talk), the world is full of examples of very famous, very talented people who were shown through door number two as children and who went on to defy expectations. But these are just the famous ones—the ones whose stories got told *after* they found exceptional success. How many kids get told "Sorry, you didn't score quite high enough on the aptitude test to get into our gifted and talented program" or "I'm afraid you didn't quite make the cut for the orchestra" or the like? If they hear this at a young age, will they have the tools to develop their talents on their own? Or will an adult help them on their journey after they walk through door number two?

Underserved Talented Kids

According to the US Department of Education Civil Rights Data Collection from 2011–2012, there were approximately 3.2 million kids enrolled in gifted and talented programs, and the selection for these programs was often done at the state and local level. In a more recent report released by Purdue University's Gifted Education Research and Resource Institute (GER2I) in 2019, approximately 3.3 million children were labeled as gifted—but 3.6 million more gifted children weren't being identified (Dreilinger 2019). According to the National Association for Gifted Children (NAGC), placement in gifted and talented programs is made through various means, including recommendations from parents and school officials, assessments, and placement exams. High-ability students from underserved populations, such as children of color and children from low-income families, are underrepresented in gifted and talented programs as well as advanced classes (2021a).

Identifying and serving underserved populations is an important undertaking. Who are the underserved? In education, this term usually means students whose needs aren't met consistently in schools: "students from culturally and linguistically diverse (CLD) backgrounds, students who are English language learners (ELL), students from a range of socioeconomic backgrounds, and twice-exceptional (2e) students" (Ritchotte, Lee, and Graefe 2020).

In sports and the arts, underrepresentation is often a socioeconomic issue. For example, high-level youth sports in the United States typically use a pay-to-play model. Some sports, such as club volleyball, soccer, and lacrosse, can cost up to ten thousand dollars a year. Common high school sports, such as football, basketball, volleyball, and soccer, usually don't require hefty fees and thus seem more accessible to all kids, socioeconomically speaking. But closer examination reveals that athletes participating in these sports often also attend year-round club programs—that is, those who can afford them and can get rides to attend these programs. This creates inequitable access to higher-level training. A similar scenario plays out in arts access for children.

It is imperative that we start to see underserved populations and serve them. Kids are often underrepresented because they are not in a school district that presents or promotes talent development programs, because they do not have adults fighting for their access to these programs, or because talent development programs are too expensive. Kids are also underrepresented because talent gatekeepers may not be watching for talent with an open mind.

> **It is imperative that we start to see underserved populations and serve them.**

I believe assessment strategies need changing—not only for underserved populations, but for all kids. In fact, the very lens through which we see and identify academic gifts and talents needs an adjustment. And this is also the case in sports, music, fine arts, and every other performance setting where kids participate.

As you read this book, I ask you to consider a new approach to defining and developing talent in children. You will see that I use examples of talent in different domains throughout the book. Obviously, I am not an expert in all these areas. But I hope you'll find that through examples and research in different performance domains, I provide a compelling case for a different approach.

CHAPTER 2
THE CONCEPT OF TALENT AS WE USE IT TODAY

In chapter 1, I listed the common current definitions of the word *talent*. Using those definitions, we can understand talent as something that is special or unique and possibly innate that helps someone do something well. In this chapter, I'll discuss how popular culture and literature in the field of talent development have recently expanded this understanding of talent to include development over time. This expansion doesn't appear to have broadened the scope of recognized talent, however. It remains largely seen as something for the few, not the many.

Talent Is Made, Not Born

If you watch or listen to any broadcast sports program, you'll probably hear the commentator talk about an athlete's talent: the athlete has speed, strength, agility, height, or other innate advantages. You'll probably also hear the pundit describe attributes that aren't innate but rather are developed over time, such as a unique skill set, hard work, focus, desire, perseverance, problem-solving, and so on. These comments suggest that talent is made, not born.

One well-researched, well-known, and fascinating book that discusses this idea is Daniel Coyle's *The Talent Code*. Coyle describes his visits to hotbeds of talent development around the

> Deep practice in the chosen field, surrounded by a supportive environment, strengthens neural pathways in the body, thus creating an effective skill or skills.

world that have churned out elite students, athletes, artists, and thinkers. One of the places Coyle visited was the Spartak Tennis Club in Moscow, Russia. He had learned that a large proportion of the world's top female tennis players trained at Spartak when they were young. Coyle also visited a Knowledge Is Power Program (KIPP) school in San Jose, California, baseball fields in the Caribbean, and soccer fields in Brazil, to name a few. In all these places, he explored these questions: *Is it the genes? Is it the training? What is it?*

Coyle's travels convinced him that talent is made, not born. He asserts that a combination of two key factors lead to talent development. **Deep practice** in the chosen field, surrounded by a

supportive environment, strengthens neural pathways in the body, thus creating an effective skill or skills. (For an in-depth discussion of deep practice, see TDZ3.)

Coyle's research makes me wonder, though. How many kids were deselected early on in each of the settings he visited? What happened to these kids? Were they actually untalented? Could they have become talented? Did they make it somewhere else? Or were they out of luck, with no chance of being identified as talented down the road?

Coyle doesn't share data on selection or follow-up in his book, but he does make clear that the talent hotbeds he visited were not broadly inclusive. They identified "talented" young athletes, artists, and students early on and did not identify others. This pattern of gatekeeping is common wherever kids are involved in performance settings.

Typical Talent Development Scenario for Kids

Let's walk through a typical kids' talent development scenario. This example is from youth sports, but similar scenarios play out in education and the arts. In this scenario, we are assembling an elite group of "talented" ten-year-old soccer players. Based on common understandings and approaches to talent, we are looking for young soccer players who are more coordinated, taller, stronger, and faster. These are often the kids who are older. Sure, they are all ten, but some are newly ten and others are nearly eleven. At this age, those months can make a big difference in perceived talent. More on this soon.

Intentionally or inadvertently, we are likely to use the Standard Model of Talent Development (SMTD). SMTD is a popular model for identifying and developing sports talent in children. (In chapter 4, I discuss Françoys Gagné's Differentiated Model of Giftedness and Talent, which is often used in academic settings.) The SMTD was coined by sports and health researchers Richard Bailey and David Collins in an article titled "The Standard Model of Talent Development and Its Discontents." In it the authors describe how many sport clubs, governing bodies, and even countries spot talented athletes and develop those athletes over time (Bailey and Collins 2013). This process is often depicted by a pyramid like the one on this page.

According to the SMTD, talent development starts at the base of the pyramid, where lots of children have the opportunity to participate in sports. Over time, the talented players are spotted as they demonstrate unique abilities or skills, and coaches offer them

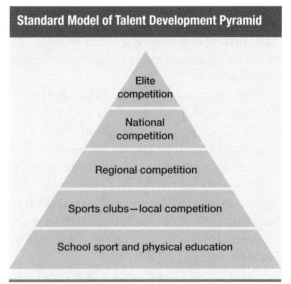

Standard Model of Talent Development Pyramid

Elite competition

National competition

Regional competition

Sports clubs—local competition

School sport and physical education

Reprinted with permission from Bailey, Richard, and David Collins. 2013. "The Standard Model of Talent Development and Its Discontents." *Kinesiology Review* 2 (4): 248–259. doi.org/10.1123/krj.2.4.248.

opportunities to move up the pyramid through ever-more-challenging competitions. This means that over time, there are fewer opportunities for everyone to develop talent. As a result, late bloomers are likely not getting as much time to practice as are children identified as talented early on.

In practice, the SMTD works like this:

- It focuses solely on progressing those identified early as talented, and not on developing talent in the wider group of participants, even though these participants may meet the criteria for progression later.

"There is no way of knowing who might have succeeded through different systems, and who were de-selected from the system but might have (under different circumstances) gone on to achieve high performance."

- Progression from one level to the next involves removal of many athletes from the developmental system or club in which they are involved.

- It presumes that early ability in an activity, which enables progression up the pyramid, predicts later success.

The SMTD is popular, but it lacks concrete evidence to support it. Bailey and Collins say, "We suggest that the apparent success of the SMTD is ultimately an optical illusion, as there is no way of knowing who might have succeeded through different systems, and who were de-selected from the system but might have (under different circumstances) gone on to achieve high performance" (2013, 249).

In other words, we can't know whether "untalented," or less talented, kids will or won't become talented as they age. Meanwhile, we select a relatively small number of "talented" kids early on and give them every opportunity to succeed. But will they be successful in the long run? And what happens if they aren't successful or eventually get deselected?

Early Talent Spotting Is No Guarantee

In the book *No Hunger in Paradise*, British sports journalist Michael Calvin discusses, among other things, early talent identification and development in English soccer academies. The book starts out with a story about a coach in South London asking a six-year-old boy, "What's your dream, son?" The boy responds, "Be a footballer." It's the right answer—the coach is looking for kids who have goals to be famous players. The book then goes on to discuss several examples of talented athletes scooped up at young ages. One is Nathaniel Clyne, who was spotted as a ten-year-old, impressed a few clubs, was traded as a youth player to a team in London, made his professional debut at seventeen, and then went on to make a lot of money after being transferred to Liverpool in 2015. Clyne was a success story. But what of other kids identified as talented in the same way?

Calvin points out that very few kids selected as talented as young players actually go on to play professionally. In fact, he says, "Since only 180 of the 1.5 million boys who play organized youth football in England at any one time become Premier League pros, the success rate is 0.012 percent" (Calvin 2017). In a chapter titled "A Parent's Warning," he tells the story of a young player identified as talented early in his life who encountered all sorts of difficulties until he hit a wall and changed course.

The kid was Kieran Bywater. He was selected at age nine to participate in a prestigious English professional football team's youth academy. Scouts and staff indicated that he was very talented. He and his parents made many sacrifices for the sport, from time spent in the car, to late nights at practices and games, to missed social events. As he got older and moved along the track toward a possible professional career, there were trials at multiple clubs, promises broken, injuries, and other tribulations culminating in Bywater breaking down in tears and leaving professional sports early in his twenties.

But what happened? Wasn't Bywater talented? Well, yes. As a child, he checked all the talent identification boxes. But he also had some bad luck along the way. Fortunately, he had an opportunity to pursue a plan B, attending a college in the United States. Bywater played college soccer at the University of Charleston, went on to play for Chattanooga FC (a lower-tier US professional soccer team), and has settled into a career as a financial planner.

But unlike Bywater, not every child has parents or coaches or other caring adults to help them pursue their talent and find out who they really are. Due to lack of know-how or lack of concern, many kids are deselected or never selected as talented—and simply don't go on to fulfill their potential.

So Is Talent Really Just More Opportunity?

So, what's the appropriate use of the word *talent*? Are early-identified kids talented, or are they simply further along the continuum of maturation for a particular domain (in arts, academics, or sports) than other kids their age are, and as a result they get more attention and practice? Are the markers for identifying talent early also markers for predicting future talent?

Innate characteristics plus deep practice leads to talent. When kids are identified as talented at an early age, they often get all kinds of extra talent development opportunities. These opportunities come in the form of better teachers and coaches, better training, extra programming, and more attention.

> Innate characteristics plus deep practice leads to talent.

As Coyle suggests, people become talented through deep practice—that is, multiple opportunities for practice. He points out in *The Talent Code* that deep practice provides opportunities for success, failure, improvement, and strengthening neural pathways. For example, elite athletes likely accumulate more deliberate practice than non-elite athletes throughout the time that they play; thus, they are more likely to maintain their elite status than a non-elite athlete is to become elite. Likewise, kids identified early as talented have doors opened for them; they are granted access and

opportunity for deep practice that the unidentified kids don't get.

Malcolm Gladwell discusses the idea of
opportunity in his book *Outliers*. Gladwell offers
an example from the Canadian youth hockey's
Major Junior A league. He points out that a
disproportionate number of kids that make the
Major Junior A teams are kids born in the first

> Self-fulfilling prophecy says that your
> expectations affect the way you treat
> a student, musician, athlete, or any
> performer.

three months of the year. In other words, these are most likely kids who are bigger, stronger, and
faster because they're a bit older than their same-age peers. Over time, due to their physical advantages, these kids have gotten extra training, more opportunities to play games, and additional time
to develop their hockey skills. Gladwell's hockey example leaves us wondering: is it a kid's "talent"
that leads to the big leagues, or is it the treatment of the child by adults during a critical time? It's
important to note, too, that the system of identification and organization in sports is designed by
adults to work for adults.

This phenomenon plays out not only in hockey but also in other sports, in the arts, and in
academics. In fact, it has a name. It's called the self-fulfilling prophecy.

Self-Fulfilling Prophecy

Self-fulfilling prophecy is the idea that higher expectations lead to higher performance and lower
expectations lead to lower performance. This concept was popularized in the 1960s by researchers
Robert Rosenthal and Lenore Jacobson. They told teachers at a public elementary school that certain of their students (identified by name) were intellectual bloomers; they had scored very well on
an (imaginary) IQ test and were going to be bright, high-achieving children. The researchers told
the teachers that the rest of the students were just ordinary kids. At the end of the year, the kids for
whom teachers had higher expectations had higher achievement, while the kids for whom teachers
had lower expectations had lower achievement (Rosenthal and Jacobson 1968).

As the Rosenthal and Jacobson study shows, early expectation can cause a belief to come true,
even if the belief is based on false information. In essence, self-fulfilling prophecy says that your
expectations affect the way you treat a student, musician, athlete, or any performer. Your treatment
then facilitates fulfillment of your expectations. This process has four steps:

1. You—as the teacher, coach, or parent—make up your mind about the likely outcomes for a
   student, performer, or athlete based on your observations of demonstrated skills, physical
   advantages, previous performances, your own experiences, and so on.

2. Your mindset affects how you interact with the kid.

3. That interaction affects the kid positively or negatively.

4. The kid performs to your expectations.

Anyone in charge of organizing kids into tiered groups in a performance setting has a particular set of weighted criteria they use to select kids. These criteria are often informed by personal experience. They may or may not rely on concrete evidence. In other words, the selection criteria can be biased, and people may not even realize it. For example, let's say I'm a basketball coach. I think short kids make good point guards, so when I'm assigning positions to the players on my team, I choose the shorter kids to play point guard. But what I am also doing is deselecting kids who aren't short based simply on my bias and with no information about their skills or desires. I've jumped headlong down the rabbit hole of self-fulfilling prophecy. My shorter players will learn how to be point guards, and my taller players won't.

I've observed that the feedback adults give to students, artists, or athletes deemed talented is often different from the feedback they give to kids deemed untalented. Talented kids may get specific, constructive feedback based on what they are doing right or wrong. Untalented kids may get general comments or encouragements, such as *keep trying* or *great effort*. Specific, constructive comments lead to improvement, as they help the child tweak the skill in question. General comments lead to improvement only if the kid can figure out what's wrong or right and tweak it on their own.

The Unselected

Early selection—or deselection—happens constantly in schools. Kids get into or don't get into gifted and talented programs all the time in classrooms across the United States. The kids who get in early on are usually students who do well in the classroom academically and on standardized tests and sometimes also those who don't have difficulty focusing or sitting still. The kids who don't get in early on may struggle in a particular subject, don't test well, and/or can't sustain focus or sit still if their lives depend on it. But just because a kid can sit still or perform well on a standardized test at age nine, does that mean they are talented and as a result will be talented in the future? On the flipside, just because a kid can't sit still or perform well on a standardized test, does that mean that they are not talented?

Let's look at a real-life example. My son was reading a book by Dav Pilkey, creator of two popular book series for kids, Captain Underpants and Dog Man. In the back of the book *Dog Man: A Tale of Two Kitties* is a blurb about the author:

> As a child, Dav Pilkey was diagnosed with dyslexia and ADHD. Dav was so disruptive in class that his teachers made him sit out in the hall every day. Luckily, Dav loved to draw and make up stories, so he spent his time in the hallway creating his own original comic books. In the second grade, Dav Pilkey created a comic book about a superhero named Captain Underpants. His teacher ripped it up and told him he couldn't spend the rest of his life making silly books. Fortunately, Dav was not a very good listener.

Fortunately, indeed.

But how did Pilkey know he had any talent for writing and drawing at all? His teachers generally sent him the message, in one way or another, "Sit outside the classroom; you are too tough to deal with."

This sort of exclusion happens often to kids, especially those who are twice exceptional (2e). Twice-exceptional children are kids who are cognitively gifted but also face learning challenges due to educational, neurodevelopmental, or mental health diagnoses. Identifying 2e kids can be difficult. Sometimes these children appear to have it all together, while at other times they appear to be struggling. Or their exceptionalities may mask each other, so neither is obvious. And once 2e kids are identified, it can be challenging to support them in ways that respect both their strengths and their special needs.

This was certainly the case for Pilkey. Throughout his childhood, the adults at school found him impossible to manage. In a news interview, he explained that the Captain Underpants characters George and Harold are both based on himself: "They don't get along very well at school, their teachers don't like them very much, their principal hates them, and that was basically my childhood." When asked if he had always wanted to become an author, Pilkey said no: "I had no idea I was good at it." It was only when he got to university that a teacher pointed out his talent. She noticed he was always drawing pictures when he was supposed to be taking notes and said, "Why don't you combine your words and your pictures and make a children's book?" Pilkey did just that—and his book was published (Sproull 2014).

Neil McCarthy, head of academy at Gloucester Rugby, and Dave Collins, professor in the School of Sport and Well Being at the University of Central Lancashire, researched what happens to deselected kids in sports. They examined young players who were deselected from a major English rugby academy when they were young. They noted that these young athletes were frequently labeled as less talented at the time of deselection due to their physical maturation. They found that among same-age players, those born later were less likely to make high-level teams as kids, but they were more likely to play professionally as they got older and more mature. The researchers surmised that these players had additional growth opportunities resulting from the challenges of being told they weren't good enough when they were young (McCarthy and Collins 2014).

Another study by three researchers at Brigham Young University also took issue with the idea that smaller, slower, less mature kids aren't talented and as a result, won't make it in sports. Benjamin Gibbs, Jonathan Jarvis, and Mikaela Dufur investigated the *Outliers* story about the disproportionate share of Canadian Major Junior A league hockey players' birthdays that fall in the first three months of the year. They looked at the National Hockey League (NHL) to examine the long-term patterns. What they found was remarkable. The effect of age on selection, or relative age effect (RAE), reverses over time. On hockey all-star and Olympic rosters, there were a balance of younger and older players, and the younger ones actually had longer careers.

> Players had additional growth opportunities resulting from the challenges of being told they weren't good enough when they were young.

Research on RAE in education has shown similar results. Data collected on older children suggests that they tend to be enrolled in gifted and talented programs more often and score higher across subject areas. Children born later in the year have been shown to achieve lower test scores (Cobley et al. 2009; Martin et al. 2004). Similar to the evidence found in sports, RAE diminishes among children as they age. The research shows this happens in both cognitive abilities and performance (Bisanz, Morrison, and Dunn 1995; Morrison, Smith, and Dow-Ehrensberger 1995; Musch and Grondin 2001).

Relative Age Effect

Relative age effect (RAE) is an important concept in early talent selection. It is the theory that among same-age kids, there are more kids on elite-level sport teams or in gifted and talented programs born in the first quarter or half of the year. So, if the age year for sports is January to December, a kid with a January birthday that year is eleven months older than a kid with a December birthday that year. An eleven-month head start carries certain likely advantages. Often kids born earlier in the year are physically larger, are stronger and faster, and have more confidence and better communication skills than the kids born later in the same year. The following diagram illustrates the physical aspect of RAE.

The advantages described here are generalizations, of course. But it's easy to see why talent selection often defaults to age. If you are building a swim squad, chess team, or orchestra that wants to excel *now*, are you going to pick the kids who are physically weaker, slower to process information, and less confident—or will you choose the stronger, faster, more self-assured ones?

| 10 years, 11 months, 364 days | 10 years, 6 months, 0 days | 10 years, 0 months, 0 days |

Evidence supports the existence of RAE in talent identification. A 2018 study of elite female soccer players showed that there was a relative age effect across all age groups studied (fourteen to eighteen years) with an overrepresentation of players born in the first three months of the year and an underrepresentation of players born in the last three months of the year (Korgaokar et al. 2018). Similar patterns appear in elite sports all over the world, from Spanish football (Jiménez and Paine 2008) to Canadian hockey (Gladwell 2008).

Classroom research has also shown a higher rate of kids in gifted and talented programs born at the beginning of the school year than at the end of the school year. A study of third graders in Israel found that older students had 3.5 times greater chance of acceptance to a gifted and talented program than younger students (Segev and Cahan 2014). In a report from Miami-Dade County Public Schools, test scores for third graders correlate directly with age. That is: kids born in September (the start of the school year) had higher average test scores than kids born in October, and so on throughout the school year, with the lowest average scores coming from those born in August (Froman and Shneydermann 2013).

So, RAE informs our understanding of talent development, but it isn't everything. Ability reflects actual growth and maturation, not only age. But how can we control for that?

In sports, some organizations are using a process called bio-banding. This means grouping athletes based on attributes associated with growth and maturation as opposed to chronological age. A young athlete's biological age is measured through predicted adult stature (PAS) and maturity offset (the estimated time needed to reach peak height velocity). Peak height velocity is the period of time when someone grows the fastest during their adolescent growth spurt. Once researchers and talent selectors group kids by biological age, they can assess from there. Currently bio-banding is used a lot in soccer, because people in the soccer world grew tired of missing smaller players who emerged to be successful elsewhere. Eventually they decided to cast a wider, more patient net. Bio-banding is now being used in other youth sports such as hockey, rugby, and baseball for the same reason: to provide opportunities for kids who are maturing at different rates than their counterparts. Advocates of bio-banding suggest that controlling for maturity variance will result in greater fairness and better results in competition, training, and selection.

Ignition

Ignition, as described by Coyle in *The Talent Code*, is that initial spark or fire stoked when one is presented with a challenge. Ignition could come from a teacher, a glimpse into one's future, a task or activity that sparks an interest, or any number of other events. Perhaps in the case of the deselected Canadian hockey players who went on to become all-stars, Olympians, or NHL players, deselection itself served as ignition. The players and their parents may have thought, "Hey, if we are here now, just think where we could be if we work at it." And then they went back to the drawing board and worked hard for the next five to ten years until they made it.

So, RAE informs our understanding of talent development, but it isn't everything. Ability reflects actual growth and maturation, not only age.

Ignition can happen anytime from anything. It could be when a child touches a basketball for the first time, or sees their first play on Broadway, or hears their first poem. Coyle points out that ignition moments are serendipitous, joyful, and followed by action. That action comes in the form of play or practice and, if it is something a child loves and is truly ignited by, it is followed by deliberate practice. This deliberate practice could be something a child does on their own, but it can also be assisted by a coach, teacher, or parent. That is to say: ignition is the start of the process, and a great talent developer serves to nurture and assist that ignition and help guide it into a blazing fire. (See **the diagram on the next page.**)

But how do we start the ignition process with kids? Doesn't everyone deserve the opportunity to have their passion ignited and cultivated? Today's difficult, slightly distracted, late-blooming child is tomorrow's potential leader, inventor, entrepreneur, opera singer, cancer curer, or star

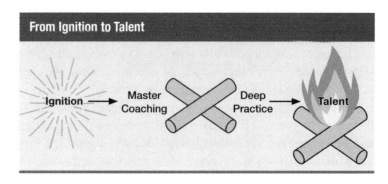

From Ignition to Talent

Ignition → Master Coaching → Deep Practice → Talent

athlete—they just need to have someone treat them as if they are. To be sure, not every kid will be the next Kamala Harris, Alex Morgan, Will Smith, Cam Newton, or Lady Gaga, but all kids can be the best versions of themselves.

I contend that talent should be a journey for all kids, not a destination for some. The journey itself is what makes up a child's current talent and leads to the future talent they will have as an adult. The rest of this book explains how talent is a lifelong pursuit and shows how we, as adults, can help kids move purposefully through that journey to make the most of their talent. Let's get to it!

CHAPTER 3
REDEFINING TALENT

In the 1987 movie *The Princess Bride*, the character Vizzini is a crime boss who overestimates his own intelligence. He repeats the word *inconceivable!* whenever he can't understand something. Eventually his underling, expert swordsman Inigo Montoya, challenges Vizzini: "You keep using that word. I do not think it means what you think it means." Montoya claims that Vizzini is using the word wrong.

This idea—that we might be using a word wrong—resonates with me. The word I think we're mishandling is *talent*. I have seen so many kids deemed untalented later become talented, over time and with support from adults. But sadly, some kids labeled as untalented are not supported in their journey. That label sticks with them. Adults look at them and treat them differently simply because someone labeled them early on.

> People like labels because they help us organize our thoughts, and institutions need cutoff lines for practical reasons. But we also need to understand the limitations of labels and cutoffs.

For me, this is inconceivable. I can't comprehend why we label so many kids at a young age and let that label steer their development. We should be defining talent in a completely different way when it comes to children. Yes, there will always be early "talent" identification and cutoff lines. People like labels because they help us organize our thoughts, and institutions need cutoff lines for practical reasons. But we also need to understand the limitations of labels and cutoffs. We need to understand what talent truly is and how we can define it differently and apply it to *all* kids.

Etymology of Talent

Knowing the history of the word *talent* can help us understand why it is used the way it is today. The various historic uses of *talent* can also help us redefine the word for future use. The concept of talent, and the word's derivatives and root words, have been around for thousands of years. The word has had several meanings over the millennia. Let's take a quick look at the etymology of the word *talent*, starting now and moving backward through time.

As we discussed in chapter 1, the first definition of *talent* in modern dictionaries is some form of the following:

- A natural ability to be good at something. (dictionary.cambridge.org)
- A special natural ability or aptitude. (dictionary.com)
- A special often athletic, creative, or artistic aptitude. (merriam-webster.com)

In late medieval Europe, *talent* meant something different. A trio of economics researchers from Spain, Belgium, and the United Kingdom explored the meaning of *talent* within the world of work (Gallardo-Gallardo, Dries, and González-Cruz 2013). They found that in the 1400s and 1500s CE, *talent* referred to people's God-given abilities, which were meant to be used to improve themselves. The belief was that all are given certain abilities, and those abilities should not be wasted but rather improved upon. These scholars also noted that earlier, in the 1200s CE, talent was seen as a feeling that makes someone want to do something (their inclination), their natural qualities (disposition), or their desire or will.

In biblical times, *talent* had nothing to do with a person's ability; it was a denomination of weight. According to Greek and Roman records, each society defined its unit of mass differently but they all used the word *talent*. For example, a Roman talent was equivalent to seventy-one pounds, while an Egyptian talent was sixty, a Babylonian talent was sixty-seven, and the Greek talent was fifty-seven pounds. Once defined, each of these units of mass was then assigned a certain value. Greater talent meant greater value. This assigned value is essentially how the word *talent* came to mean "money."

This use of the word *talent* as a denomination of weight came from the Greek word *tálanton*, which means "a scale of balance, a balance, a pair of scales, or that which is weighed." *Tálanton* in turn derived from the word *tlao*, which means "to bear." The word *tlao* is equivalent to the Greek word *phero*, which means the following:

- to endure the rigor of a thing, to bear patiently one's conduct, or to abstain from punishing or destroying
- to carry some burden or to uphold or keep from falling
- to bring forward or apply

I find it interesting that the concept of talent includes what weight we assign to the talent. Somewhere along the line in each society, people decided to weight how much each talent was worth. This weight in turn granted certain importance to each talent, giving it less or more monetary value.

This resembles the way modern society weights certain early talents in academics, sports, or any other performance setting. Those weighted talents then are looked for, coveted, and selected.

The Problem with Labels and Cutoffs

We need to redefine the word *talent* because the label has too much power. What happens when children are *not* labeled as talented? Some children are able to embrace the *untalented* label; they recognize their weaknesses and work on strengthening those areas. Or if they're lucky enough to have a comfortable socioeconomic status or attentive adults in their corner, they get lots of other chances.

But some kids don't have any of these assets. What of those kids? What about that which they bear and carry in themselves—their will, their inclinations, and their natural abilities? Do those just vanish? How can they make it in the world? Kids, like all people, are works in progress. And kids count on adults to assist them in this work, to help them develop who they are.

We need to redefine the word *talent* because the label has too much power.

We adults owe it to kids to not let labels and other adult constructs limit them. For the most part, kids are just chugging along trying to learn and get better at stuff. Then at some point, adults label kids for pragmatic reasons. But is that the best approach? Adult labels may energize some kids, but they may redirect or derail the progress of other kids. I think we need a new approach to talent that serves the children, not the adults.

Talent Is a Process

Talent is innate ability that can be improved. The talent that kids bear needs to be guided and assisted as it develops over time. In other words, it is a process.

When we talk about talent in people, we often say things like *they are so smart* or *wow, she is fast* or *that guy is incredibly strong*. Such qualities can be built, to some extent. Sometimes we talk about talent in slightly different ways: *she is hypercompetitive* or *they just don't quit* or *he has ice in his veins* or *she can just dial in and focus*. These abilities might seem more innate. Which kind of ability is more important? Neither—because talent is a process. What one has (abilities, inclinations) to begin with is important, and what a person does (effort, learning) with their raw materials over time is just as important.

Think about developing your own talents as an adult. When you are trying to get better at something, you are developing a talent. You believe you'll get better if you learn and work hard enough. All you need is a chance to do that work.

When we adults talk about our talents, we tend to refer to them as things we're good at. That almost always means we've developed them over time. They were probably personal passions and therefore things we were decent at to begin with. We spent many hours and a lot of effort improving our skills and navigating struggles. Others assisted us in navigating our failures and doubts as we made our way, but because we are adults, with years of experience and self-knowledge, we can make choices and course corrections independently, with a certain amount of wisdom.

> ❝
>
> The pursuit of talent is talent itself.
> Talent is what EVERY child bears and
> carries and brings forth over time.

Kids, on the other hand, are still developing cognitively, emotionally, and physically. They may struggle to make informed choices on their journey. That's why they need adults to help them.

For adults, helping children develop their talent is about balancing failures and successes. It means keeping an open mind. Children push boundaries in order to discover and develop their abilities. When we see them act out or make problematic choices, we need to help them correct their behavior or learn how to make better choices without squashing their spirit. Talent is a journey, not a destination—and kids who are on this journey deserve the opportunity to get there, wherever their "there" is.

I propose a working definition of talent in children that not only allows people to view talent as a journey but also provides a vision of talent as a journey for *all* kids, not just some. This working definition should tell adults, "Hey, keep an open mind. Help those kids who've been told they're untalented figure out how to develop to their full potential." It should also tell children that **the pursuit of talent is talent itself**. *Talent is what EVERY child bears and carries and brings forth over time.*

CHAPTER 4
REAPPROACHING TALENT DEVELOPMENT IN KIDS

In the late 1930s and early 1940s, Maya Angelou was a little girl who experienced a series of traumas. Through these traumas, she came to believe that her voice was dangerous and that it could hurt people, so she chose not to speak for five years. This made school difficult for her. Because she didn't talk, her classmates and teachers assumed she was stupid. But her grandmother, whom she called Momma, knew better and said so: "Momma don't care what these people say, that you must be an idiot, a moron, 'cause you can't talk. Momma don't care. Momma know that when you and the good Lord get ready, you gon' be a teacher" (Moore 2003). Eventually a patient, persistent, observant teacher took the time with young Angelou to nurture her voice, asking her to read poetry aloud. At thirteen, she began speaking again at the behest of the teacher, who said to her, "You do not love poetry, not until you speak it" (Street 2017).

Most of us know stories like this, about successful people who were told as kids that they weren't good enough. Some of these kids pick themselves up, dust themselves off, and get after it on their own. Other kids are given a second chance or placed in an environment that says "We got this. Here's what we need to do." In both scenarios, kids find their way toward improvement somehow. I wish this were the case for all kids. But many kids don't know the route to talent, aren't given a map, don't have support, or face a bunch of roadblocks that seem insurmountable to a kid.

Talent is both innate and learned. No one knows what percentage is innate and what percentage is learned. More importantly, no one knows what help a kid will get from someone else over time. That's why it's important to better understand talent development in kids and then use this understanding to reapproach talent development and talent identification. Talent takes many forms and develops on many timelines. We adults—as teachers, coaches, and program leaders—have a role to play in developing talent in every kid.

> Many kids don't know the route to talent, aren't given a map, don't have support, or face a bunch of roadblocks that seem insurmountable to a kid.

Gagné's Model: Talent Development in the 10 Percent

Gagné's Differentiated Model of Giftedness and Talent depicts how skills and abilities equate to talent in educational contexts (Gagné 1999). See **the chart below.**

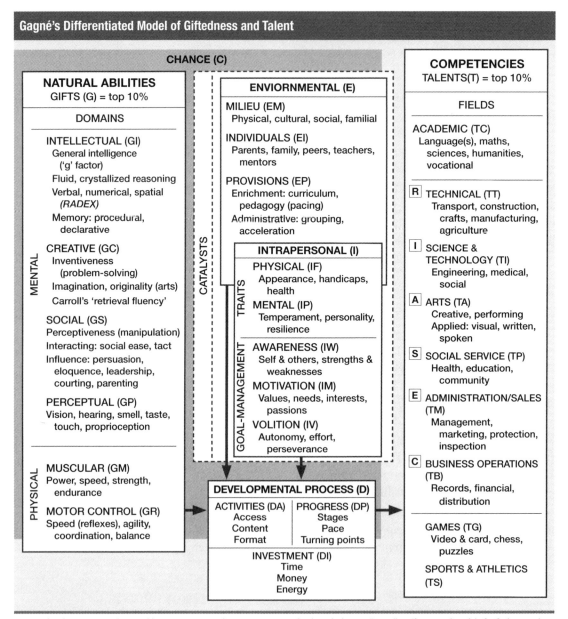

Gagné's Differentiated Model of Giftedness and Talent

CHANCE (C)

NATURAL ABILITIES
GIFTS (G) = top 10%

DOMAINS

MENTAL

INTELLECTUAL (GI)
General intelligence
('g' factor)
Fluid, crystallized reasoning
Verbal, numerical, spatial
(RADEX)
Memory: procedural,
declarative

CREATIVE (GC)
Inventiveness
(problem-solving)
Imagination, originality (arts)
Carroll's 'retrieval fluency'

SOCIAL (GS)
Perceptiveness (manipulation)
Interacting: social ease, tact
Influence: persuasion,
eloquence, leadership,
courting, parenting

PERCEPTUAL (GP)
Vision, hearing, smell, taste,
touch, proprioception

PHYSICAL

MUSCULAR (GM)
Power, speed, strength,
endurance

MOTOR CONTROL (GR)
Speed (reflexes), agility,
coordination, balance

CATALYSTS

ENVIORNMENTAL (E)

MILIEU (EM)
Physical, cultural, social, familial

INDIVIDUALS (EI)
Parents, family, peers, teachers,
mentors

PROVISIONS (EP)
Enrichment: curriculum,
pedagogy (pacing)
Administrative: grouping,
acceleration

INTRAPERSONAL (I)

TRAITS

PHYSICAL (IF)
Appearance, handicaps,
health

MENTAL (IP)
Temperament, personality,
resilience

GOAL-MANAGEMENT

AWARENESS (IW)
Self & others, strengths &
weaknesses

MOTIVATION (IM)
Values, needs, interests,
passions

VOLITION (IV)
Autonomy, effort,
perseverance

DEVELOPMENTAL PROCESS (D)

ACTIVITIES (DA)	PROGRESS (DP)
Access	Stages
Content	Pace
Format	Turning points

INVESTMENT (DI)
Time
Money
Energy

COMPETENCIES
TALENTS(T) = top 10%

FIELDS

ACADEMIC (TC)
Language(s), maths,
sciences, humanities,
vocational

R TECHNICAL (TT)
Transport, construction,
crafts, manufacturing,
agriculture

I SCIENCE &
TECHNOLOGY (TI)
Engineering, medical,
social

A ARTS (TA)
Creative, performing
Applied: visual, written,
spoken

S SOCIAL SERVICE (TP)
Health, education,
community

E ADMINISTRATION/SALES
(TM)
Management,
marketing, protection,
inspection

C BUSINESS OPERATIONS
(TB)
Records, financial,
distribution

GAMES (TG)
Video & card, chess,
puzzles

SPORTS & ATHLETICS
(TS)

Reprinted with permission of Sage Publications Inc. Journals. From Association for the Gifted. 1999. "Gagné's Differentiated Model of Giftedness and Talent (DMGT)." *Journal for the Education of the Gifted* 22 (2): 230–234. doi.org/10.1177/016235329902200209. Permission conveyed through Copyright Clearance Center, Inc.

Gagné's model defines *gifts* as natural abilities in a domain that place a child among the top 10 percent of their same-age peers in that domain (Gagńe 1985). The model shows the idea that people enter a talent development pathway with gifts in any of several domains (their natural physical and mental abilities). People transform these gifts, through learning and practice via teaching or coaching, into talents (competencies in several fields). Gifts are what kids theoretically start out with, but even Gagné himself is quick to point out that these gifts, while easy to see in children, are changeable. He says it's these high natural abilities that some people call "talent" (Gagné 1999).

A child comes in with gifts—mental or physical abilities—and a nurturing environment helps shape these gifts. It is this interaction that leads to talent.

The middle section of Gagné's model is especially interesting. In this section, intrapersonal catalysts (nature) and environmental catalysts (nurture) interact in the developmental process. Put simply, a child comes in with gifts—mental or physical abilities—and a nurturing environment helps shape these gifts. It is this interaction that leads to talent, provided there are gifts in the first place.

Gagné points out that the intrapersonal catalysts are influenced by genetics. He suggests that qualities such as motivation and desire play a major role in guiding and sustaining talent through failure, temporary setbacks, and other obstacles in the process of talent development. Temperament, traits, and disorders can either support and inspire or derail talent development.

Environmental catalysts are critical to talent development. Gagné suggests that many people and things influence talent, both positively and negatively. Not only parents and teachers, but also peers and siblings, play a part.

Gagné offers ideas and research findings that can help us understand talent identification and development in education, sports, the arts, or any performance endeavor in which a child might participate.

I do think Gagné's model provides a viable explanation of talent development. But I take issue with the notion of a "top 10 percent."

Growth Mindset as Environmental Catalyst

Growth mindset is discussed in TDZ1, but it's important to briefly mention here that it is a key catalyst. Growth mindset is a concept introduced by Carol Dweck, a renowned psychology professor at Stanford University. The crux of her theory is that people who have a growth mindset believe their abilities and skills can change with hard work and deliberate practice. Conversely, people who have a fixed mindset think their abilities are innate and can't change. People who surround a child (teachers, coaches, parents, relatives, and so on) can influence the child's mindset and—ideally—help them develop a growth mindset that will stay with them for life.

Who is to say that only the top 10 percent of kids who are considered to have gifts in a domain at a particular moment—and only these kids—should get a chance at talent development and all its benefits? One moment of measurement cannot be the deciding factor in a kid's talent journey.

What About the Other 90 Percent?

I am well aware that not everyone can be in a gifted and talented program, but a cutoff line of giftedness at 10 percent is arbitrary. In any group of one hundred children ranked by "gifts," is child number eleven automatically not gifted, untalented? Let's say it's your child. And at the time of giftedness assessment, your child has difficulty focusing or is nervous or is going through a growth spurt.

Also, at what age are we measuring the top 10 percent? At ten years old? Thirteen years old? Sixteen years old? Your kid's talent may in fact cross the 10 percent threshold sometime, but if it happens too late, your kid is out of luck because they weren't "gifted and talented" at the time of testing.

Of course, accurate talent prediction is impossible. Maturational growth plays a major role in talent development. In addition, what makes a performer great at age seventeen in the current state of the activity won't necessarily be the same in twenty years, because tactics change, preferred skills change, and so forth.

> Children do not develop along a steady, straightforward path. This is why we must be more open-minded in our understanding of talent.

Children do not develop along a steady, straightforward path. If you examine the progression to success of current high-level academics, artists, and athletes, you'll see many long, winding, unpredictable journeys with all kinds of ups and downs. In other words, their development has been nonlinear. In fact, I suggest this notion—that development is nonlinear—is the heart of the reason why we must be more open-minded in our understanding of talent. If our understanding of talent is too narrow, we run the risk of completely missing the unselected many while focusing on the selected few.

Many ideas used in kids' schooling, sports, and other performance endeavors are valid and reliable; however, many ideas are not. "Stickiness," an idea coined by Malcolm Gladwell in his book *The Tipping Point*, applies here. Stickiness is when ideas are embraced and become popular—regardless of whether they have concrete evidence or measurable results. A related idea, "scienciness," is used by Dave Collins and Áine MacNamara in their book *Talent Development: A Practitioner Guide* to refer to "the illusion of scientific credibility and validity that provides a degree of authority to otherwise dubious ideas" (2018, 10). Scienciness makes pseudoscientific sticky ideas, such as the ten-thousand-hour rule or early specialization in sport, seem scientific. These ideas take on a life of their own, become widespread, and may or may not translate into talent for the performer.

Collins and McNamara suggest that practitioners in talent identification and development should ask questions, weigh the evidence, and make well-informed, thoughtful decisions relevant to their context. I think that's good advice: use what works, and ignore what doesn't. In my opinion, what doesn't work in Gagné's model is its approach to the identification of talent. What does work is its approach to the development of talent.

The Developmental Process: How It Is and How It Can Be

The middle section of Gagné's model discusses the process that occurs as kids move along the talent development pathway. Environmental and intrapersonal catalysts play critical roles in this process. Viewed through a nature-versus-nurture lens, intrapersonal catalysts are factors within the nature of a person. They are traits that a person carries into the talent development process. But as Gagné points out, these traits are highly malleable in children and are influenced by the environment. Nature is important, but nature is always susceptible to nurture—especially in kids.

But just how much can the environment (nurture) impact the intrapersonal (nature)? *No one knows.*

If we accept that the environment plays a key role in the middle section of the model—that nature affects nurture in the developmental process—then shouldn't we also entertain the possibility that the environment impacts giftedness as well? Is giftedness really as limited as Gagné's model suggests? Why not open the idea of giftedness to more than the top 10 percent? After all, our brains and our bodies are continually changing and are continually impacted by our environment, positively and negatively.

The human brain is a remarkable organ. It has the capacity to adapt to changing environmental stimuli, something scientists call *plasticity*. Plasticity enables us to learn from the environment at any age. To fully understand this ability and to connect it to talent development in children, we need to distinguish between experience-*dependent* plasticity and experience-*expectant* plasticity:

Equity in Talent Development

I want to take a moment to talk about the importance of creating talent development environments for *all* kids, not just kids who grow up in certain school districts or who can afford, or can get a ride to, or have time for extracurricular activities. If we believe that nurture can impact nature, and that environments are a major catalyst in this nurturing process, then it's imperative that we create these environments for underserved populations, such as those discussed in chapter 1.

As you move through this book, you'll find tangible ideas to help you develop talent in kids. We all need to do a better job of making sure we reach as many children as possible. Talent exists in all kids and can be developed anywhere.

- **Experience-dependent plasticity** is the brain's ability to adapt to new information. This ability underlies learning at any age. It is the brain's readiness to respond to stimuli in the environment.

- **Experience-expectant plasticity** refers to the brain's ability to integrate environmental stimuli into the normal patterns of development. Certain environmental exposures during limited "sensitive periods" of development are critical for healthy maturation.

Notice the first word in each of these concepts: *experience*. The key to development is, of course, getting some experience. And the critical difference between the two types of plasticity that enable development is *when* the stimuli happen.

The sensitive period—the *when*—in experience-expectant plasticity has to do with a person's critical learning period for a particular skill, or the time during which a person would learn the skill best. Language learning offers a good example of this. For a person to develop a particular accent or recognize certain sounds, they need exposure to the language in question during the first years of life—the sensitive period for language learning.

During a sensitive period, synapses (connections between neurons) in the brain are pruned and strengthened. After this sensitive period, fewer changes to synapses can occur. So, for example, while you can learn a language after the sensitive period for language learning, perhaps you cannot learn it to the fullest, and learning the language may prove more difficult than it would have been in your early years.

Cognitive scientists have been studying the brain of infants and young children and are learning more and more about sensitive periods. For example, the sensitive period for motor learning and sensory processing is actually all throughout childhood. Knowing this can strongly influence our giftedness gatekeeping methods. Kids can learn a lot of information and skills if they are worked with and given plenty of stimuli during this sensitive period, right? Can't kids with lower-level gifts labeled untalented still possibly become talented if provided with opportunities through the environment to make the most of experience-expectant plasticity?

Yes, they can. In fact, a study by Sarah-Jayne Blakemore highlights the critical importance of providing educational interventions well into late adolescence in order to take advantage of plasticity. She showed that adolescents made massive improvements on a verbal reasoning test after weeks and weeks of learning opportunities. Eleven-to-thirteen-year-olds improved some, but sixteen-to-eighteen-year-olds made the biggest improvements (Blakemore 2018).

Adolescents aged eleven to eighteen improved their verbal reasoning with training! Working with kids during these critical sensitive periods can yield significant benefits. So shouldn't we advocate for an environment rich in experience-expectant plasticity opportunities in order to foster giftedness and talent for all children, not just the top 10 percent?

Yes, we should. Experience-producing drive (EPD) theory can help explain why the environment makes a difference in development. EPD theory says that human beings are active agents designed to survive in their environment, and as such, they've evolved traits to facilitate their survival. These traits lead people to create and seek out physical and mental environments compatible with their genes. In other words, we influence ourselves (by our motivations, desires, preferences, and so on), and those influences lead us to seek experiences in things we are doing and things we like doing. These experiences that we choose lead us to pursue, practice, and acquire skills that help us get better at the things we are motivated to pursue.

For example, if you like hearing the clarinet (because you were exposed to the clarinet when you were young), and you enjoy playing the clarinet, you will likely seek out experiences that help you be good at playing the clarinet. Maybe as a child you also got positive feedback about playing the clarinet. EPD theory suggests that this feedback, combined with your enjoyment in hearing and playing the clarinet, drives you on to get more experiences and opportunities with the clarinet. Throughout this *driven* process to *produce experience*, you try to surround yourself with as many high-quality environmental circumstances as you can to reinforce your desires (Kaufman 2013).

Researchers suggest that genes do influence small individual differences in capacity as well as sensitivity to things that individuals learn (Johnson 2013). That is to say, kids are genetically predisposed to pay attention to, and as a result learn from, different environmental stimuli. For example, some kids enjoy music, and some kids

To reach the most kids and develop the most talent, we must create environments and give opportunities.

enjoy math, and as a result perhaps they may understand and pursue those things with more passion. But researchers are also quick to point out that how kids express this drive is likely dependent on being exposed to the right situation at the right time. If they are not exposed to environmental stimuli at the right time, their development could be hindered.

Talent researcher Wendy Johnson contributes a chapter to the book *The Complexity of Greatness*. In it she talks a great deal about EPD theory and ties it to talent and the pursuit of greatness. She asserts that the innately talented differ little in ability potential from the innately ordinary. However, the innately talented may differ in the drive or motivation that they have to pursue greatness (Johnson 2013).

Johnson does not shy away from the idea that genes play a part in talent, and neither do I. But as we digest EPD theory and all the other available evidence on talent development, I think we should consider the fact that, by and large, we don't know *exactly* who has what genes; when the best time to identify and ignite that gene might be; and when that ignited gene will come to fruition. Therefore, to reach the most kids and develop the most talent, we must create environments and give opportunities.

I have seen schools and organizations that have set talent identification cutoffs at the proverbial 10 percent. I have also seen schools and organizations that have expanded cutoffs well beyond 10 percent to cast a wider net; they take a proactive approach to developing talent in the many as opposed to the few. I have seen both approaches produce higher achievement. How can this be? In the places where I have visited, interviewed, researched, or participated that have produced better athletes, students, musicians, and performers of all kinds, it's not the method of identifying talent that's better. Rather, *the environment is better*. It's richer in opportunities *for all*. Those opportunities allow everyone, even the "untalented," to develop their talent.

PART 2

Talent Development Zones

Talent cannot be predicted, and research shows that the environment is a critical determinant in the development of talent. So, how can parents, teachers, and coaches of kids create environments rich in opportunities for *all* kids to develop talent? To address this need, I have compiled and organized ten evidence-based, developmentally appropriate strategies called Talent Development Zones (TDZs). These TDZs take the concepts and research we've explored and transform them into practical strategies adults can use to create environments that help kids develop their talents:

1. Embrace failure as an opportunity.
2. Smash ceilings.
3. Provide opportunities for deep, deliberate practice.
4. Build realistic optimism.
5. Foster in kids a love for their endeavors.
6. Develop and inspire creativity.
7. Build "I can" kids.
8. Help kids manage pressure.
9. Develop grit (and know when to change course).
10. Create a culture of development.

In the following chapters, I define each TDZ, discuss the research behind it, and share stories about people who have used this concept to help develop kids' talent. Then I provide tangible things adults can do to create that great environment—that Talent Development Zone—for kids. This isn't a recipe book for creating superstars; rather, it offers lots of suggestions you can use to *help children develop themselves.*

EMBRACE FAILURE AS AN OPPORTUNITY

In 2001, seven-year-old Harry Kane signed a soccer academy contract at the famed English Premier League club Arsenal. He played one season with Arsenal—only to be cut at the end of the season because he was too "chubby" (Moses 2018). At age eleven he signed with crosstown rival Tottenham and has played there ever since. Today he's considered one of the world's best strikers and is famous for his prolific goal scoring.

Kane says the experience of failure was the best thing that ever happened to him. But of course at the time, it was devastating. His road to success was a long and winding one. The years between 2001 and today were filled with disappointment, more failures, loan spells at different clubs, and difficult times. But he had made a choice—and so had those around him—to embrace the failure as an opportunity and get on with the work of improvement.

Understanding Failure

Kids fail all the time. They might get bad grades, might not make the team or program or play they were striving for, might mess up on the field or onstage. It hurts. And yet, failure is so good for kids. They don't have to like it. But if they think about their failure, learn from it, and go after their goal again—in other words, if they embrace failure—it becomes an opportunity.

When kids fall, are they willing to get up and try again? Do they know that trying again is an option? Do they know how to get up or what to do after they get up?

After failing at something, kids need someone to say, "You aren't there *yet*. But that doesn't mean you won't get there. If you work hard and improve and try again later, in time you *will* get there." As adults and talent developers, we must be the ones to say that.

> "
> Failure is so good for kids. They don't have to like it. But if they think about their failure, learn from it, and go after their goal again—in other words, if they embrace failure—it becomes an opportunity.

Remember our discussion on experience-producing drive (EPD) theory in chapter 4? EPD theory says people need to *want* to do certain things in order to develop those abilities; they must seek environments that help them succeed. But here's the catch: they also need to know those environments exist in the first place. And then they need access to those environments. For kids, that knowledge and access depends on the adults around them.

Growth Mindset

Adults need to help kids adopt a growth mindset. Chapter 4 introduced the concept of growth mindset as an environmental catalyst in developing talent. Let's explore growth mindset (and its opposite, fixed mindset) in more depth.

When people have a growth mindset, they believe their skills and abilities—in other words, their talents—are changeable. As kids try to develop their talents, they will make lots of mistakes and experience many failures. A growth mindset enables kids to keep trying, to grow and improve over time.

When people have a fixed mindset, they view mistakes and failures as evidence that they are not smart or gifted or talented. They believe their abilities are innate and cannot change. A fixed mindset may lead a child to not try their hardest for fear of failing, and feeling like *they are a failure* (and will always be) instead of understanding that *they failed* (but can improve).

Nobody has a growth mindset or a fixed mindset 100 percent of the time. Sometimes you may believe you have great potential, and you can see that setbacks are just part of the process of learning and improving. Other times you may believe your weaknesses limit you, and you feel like giving up at the first setback. Dweck says, "We're all a mixture of fixed and growth mindsets, we will probably always be, and if we want to move closer to a growth mindset in our thoughts and practices, we need to stay in touch with our fixed-mindset thoughts and deeds" (2015).

Dweck's research shows that mindset develops early in life. In one study she and her colleagues found that four-year-olds showed their growth or fixed mindset in their approach to jigsaw puzzles. After completing an easy puzzle, some kids chose to try more difficult puzzles, while others chose to redo the easy puzzle. In other words, some kids

GROWTH VERSUS FIXED MINDSET

When people have a **growth mindset**:

- They view failures or mistakes as opportunities to grow.
- They like to try new things or new ways to improve.
- They believe their effort and their attitude determine their ability.
- They view feedback as helpful.
- They get inspired by other people's successes.

When people have a **fixed mindset**:

- They view failures or mistakes as permanent.
- They don't like to try new things; they stick to what they know.
- They believe their abilities are predetermined and can't change.
- They take feedback and criticism personally.
- They give up when they're frustrated.

(with a growth mindset) wanted to test themselves, whereas some kids (with a fixed mindset) wanted to make sure they could succeed in order to show their intelligence (Dweck 2016, 16–17).

So, can we help kids develop a growth mindset? Yes—and constructive praise is one great way to do that. Constructive praise is praising kids for their effort (when warranted) instead of their abil-

> When children are struggling, adults should keep providing constructive feedback and opportunities to try again to help foster a growth mindset.

ity (getting the right answer, mastering the skill, winning, or simply being "smart" or "talented"). For example, when a child tries a new skill, an adult might say, "I like the way you practiced that, and I see you are improving."

But continually praising effort when a child continually gets it all wrong is not a helpful strategy. Making mistakes—and managing those mistakes—is important in developing a growth mindset. When children are struggling, adults should keep providing constructive feedback and opportunities to try again (revise the paper, try the skill differently) to help foster a growth mindset. Some children may have difficulty learning from their own failures. It can be hard to focus on their own weaknesses and missteps. But even in these cases, children can usually learn from the mistakes of others (Eskreis-Winkler 2021). To help us understand why mistakes can be helpful and how adults can create an environment that allows kids to make the most of their mistakes, let's look at Dweck's research on motivation.

Achievement Goal Theory: Process Versus Product

Early in her career, Dweck was a faculty member at the University of Illinois, where cutting-edge research on motivation and children took place. One product of this research was achievement goal theory (AGT). AGT provides many of the theoretical underpinnings of growth mindset and can point us toward some practical approaches to developing growth mindset in children.

According to AGT, people judge themselves successful in performance settings in one of two ways. Some people feel they've succeeded when they give effort or improve; they are "task" or "mastery" oriented. Other people feel they've succeeded when they win or beat other people; they are "ego" or "performance" oriented. When task-oriented individuals fail, they get up and try again. When ego-oriented people fail, they make excuses, quit, or engage in maladaptive coping strategies.

Researchers have used AGT to investigate and explain children's perceptions of success in sport and education. This research has shown that kids tend to think in one of these ways (Harwood, Spray, and Keegan 2008):

- If they are **process oriented** (task or mastery oriented), they are focused on improving and learning. They judge success based on their own improvement.

- If they are **product oriented** (ego or performance oriented), they are focused on winning and beating others. They judge success based on their achievement compared to others; they feel like they've failed if they lose.

People can have both orientations. The best athletes, students, artists, businesspeople, and competitors in any field are usually both process and product oriented. They want to improve, and they also want to win or get a high score or beat other people. Problems tend to happen when people are focused more on product than process. When the going gets tough, they may cheat. They may get anxious and have no coping skills. They may not want to improve or learn what it takes to get better. In other words, they do not persist. They often quit.

AGT says that while children bring certain orientations to their endeavors, people who surround children create climates that can influence these orientations and even change them over time. Parents, teachers, and coaches create climates that reward success in different ways:

- Some adults create a **product environment**. They stress winning and beating others above all else. They ask, "Did you win?" or "Did you get an A?" or imply, "If you didn't win (or get an A), you failed."

- Some adults create a **process environment**. They stress working and trying hard. They reward effort and improvement. They teach children to measure success relative to themselves, not others.

An adult who creates a product environment says to kids: winning or getting the top grade is the most important thing. This is unsustainable because everybody fails at some point. And when kids don't win in a product environment, they enjoy the activity less, get anxious, get frustrated instead of looking for solutions, and don't persist. Striving to be the best isn't inherently bad, but being the best is a lot of pressure on a kid and often is not within a kid's control.

Mindset and Environment in Action

In sports: An athlete has success at a young age because she matures early. She doesn't practice skills much, but she still wins a lot. Her coach praises her wins instead of her efforts. As the child gets older, she loses repeatedly to an athlete she's beaten plenty of times before. The opponent's coach has praised the kid's efforts and encouraged continued practice in the face of losses. This child understands that winning is great, but there is more to the sport than winning, and she must persist to improve her skills. The early maturer, on the other hand, has no coping skills because she has always won easily. When push comes to shove in a competition, she gets anxious, enjoys it less, and eventually quits.

In school: A student is selected for a gifted and talented program because he is a really good test taker and a high achiever in math. Because of his math scores, he doesn't practice math skills very much. He continues to do well in math until he enters high school. He is placed in advanced geometry and gets a C on his first test. His friend in the same class, who does okay in math because he studies a lot, also gets a C. The studier's parents have always encouraged him to work his hardest and tell him a C is okay, but also ask him if he did his best and ask how they might help him do better. Meanwhile, the parents of the early high achiever come down hard on him. Because he has never really had to study, he first makes excuses, and then to protect his ego, he decides he just wasn't meant to do well and gives up.

Instead, adults can create climate of persistence in the face of competition and adversity. Dweck urges us to create a process environment. If we stress working hard, trying new skills, and getting up after being knocked down, we will be developing children who believe their success is due to effort (as opposed to innate, unchangeable ability), who enjoy their endeavors, and who are determined and resilient.

Scenarios like those in the "Mindset and Environment in Action" sidebar play out all the time in school, the arts, sports, and every performance domain where kids participate. Early achievers who never experience failure often don't understand what it means to dig in and work hard to improve, especially if they—or the adults and environments around them—are product oriented or have fixed mindsets. Whereas less-developed athletes, performers, and students who are supported in growth mindsets and a focus on process tend to work hard all the time, regardless of their achievements.

TDZ1 To-Do List

To create a Talent Development Zone that helps kids embrace failure as an opportunity, adults need to:

- emphasize working hard over being the best
- view mistakes as chances to grow
- encourage kids to try new things
- use comparisons wisely

Emphasize Working Hard over Being the Best

Let's be clear: being the best isn't bad. But by definition, not everyone can be the best. And if it is the only thing children are focused on, and there's no attention to improving, then we have a problem. After all, what happens if they aren't the best—or aren't always the best? Do they quit, or can they keep on keeping on?

When kids fail—and when they succeed—adults should emphasize and reward their hard work. Rewarding kids for their effort offers them autonomy and a bit of control over what is going on, and it deemphasizes comparisons and competition with other people. Here are some examples of adults emphasizing effort:

- A child comes home with a grade that isn't an A. Find out if they've given their best effort and if so, reward them for that. If they haven't, talk about why not and see how they might feel motivated or supported to work harder—or smarter—next time.
- A child has lost a game but has given their all. Praise them for that.

- A child gets a score of 94 in a piano contest while a friend gets a 98. The child is upset. Try to find out why the child is upset. (For example: "I can see you're upset. Let's talk about it.") If it is because they got a lower score than their friend, take the emphasis off the friend and help the child focus on self-improvement instead.

View Mistakes as Chances to Grow

When children make mistakes or fail in their endeavors, they're often sad or mad about it. We can help them manage or change those thoughts and feelings. Tell kids that mistakes and failures are simply opportunities to get better. Say, "Let's see what we're missing and then do something about it." Here are some examples:

- A child tries out for a select team and doesn't make it. Instead of focusing on the failure, talk about how this is an opportunity. Find out what the coach thinks is missing from the child's skill set and try to improve it. You might even encourage the kid to try out for a different team.

- A child doesn't make the cut on a test to enter the gifted and talented program at school. Find out where the child fell short and say, "If you want to improve these areas and try again, we can work on them together."

Encourage Kids to Try New Things

Sometimes when kids fail, they get back up and try it again. But perhaps they were trying the wrong approach. Embracing failure doesn't mean that a child has to keep taking the same path. Failing offers an opportunity to try a new approach that perhaps they hadn't yet considered. For example: A child auditions for the school musical and doesn't get the part. Talk about new paths, such as auditioning for a different type of production, choosing different audition pieces, or working on stage presence and confidence.

Use Comparisons Wisely

Often when kids fail, they or the adults around them compare them to kids who've succeeded. Comparisons can be counterproductive. When kids compare themselves to others and chalk up others' success to coveted inborn characteristics, kids conclude that success is out of their own reach. The coveting child may be correct in the case of physical size or strength, but skills aren't inborn—especially at a young age. Skills can be developed.

However, comparisons are not always bad. It depends on what is being compared. If you are looking at *how* another kid succeeded, and you are going to use that information to improve, then great! Here are a couple of examples:

- A kid you coach didn't make an elite travel team, while another young athlete did. Your player says the other athlete is just fast or strong and doesn't work hard enough to deserve it, perhaps lashing out or making excuses. You can take this opportunity to ask your player if they did everything they could have done to make that team. Perhaps you can also talk about how that other athlete was training extra after school and working out independently, and that these are things your player could also do to prepare for trying again next year.

- A girl in your child's class got 95 percent on a test, and your child got 90 percent. Your child (who tends to be ego or performance oriented) feels like a failure because her friend got a higher grade. Your child asks to speak with the teacher at lunchtime. She is fixated on the comparison instead of the reasons behind the scores. You can tell your child that students who tend to do really well on tests tend to study, take notes, and prepare for class, and that she can do all these things to give her the best chance of improving her grade.

Remember: there is value in a skinned knee. We want to help heal it, of course, but we should learn from it as well. Consider these words of wisdom from US Supreme Court Chief Justice John Roberts, delivered to his son's class as they graduated from middle school (Reilly 2017):

> From time to time in the years to come, I hope you will be treated unfairly, so that you will come to know the value of justice. I hope that you will suffer betrayal because that will teach you the importance of loyalty. Sorry to say, but I hope you will be lonely from time to time so that you don't take friends for granted. I wish you bad luck, again, from time to time so that you will be conscious of the role of chance in life and understand that your success is not completely deserved and that the failure of others is not completely deserved either. And when you lose, as you will from time to time, I hope every now and then, your opponent will gloat over your failure. It is a way for you to understand the importance of sportsmanship. I hope you'll be ignored so you know the importance of listening to others, and I hope you will have just enough pain to learn compassion. Whether I wish these things or not, they're going to happen. And whether you benefit from them or not will depend upon your ability to see the message in your misfortunes.

TDZ2
SMASH CEILINGS

A ceiling is:

- the inside top part or covering of a room, opposite the floor
- any overhanging expanse seen from below
- an upper limit set on anything, as by official regulation

Understanding Ceilings

Having a ceiling on your home is a good thing. It keeps the elements out, the heat or cold in, and the belongings in the house safe. But when a ceiling is an upper limit set on kids' skills and abilities, it's not so great. It blocks the growth of the person beneath it. This is exactly what we don't want when it comes to kids developing their talent.

Often when we consider kids and their talent, we think about how far they can go with it. When children are selected or given opportunities in arts, academics, or sports, both children and the adults around them start to imagine the possibilities. They may dream about college scholarships or professional opportunities and have visions of twenty years down the road. When kids are identified as talented, the possibilities seem limitless; there's no ceiling in sight.

> When a ceiling is an upper limit set on kids' skills and abilities, it blocks the growth of the person beneath it.

When kids aren't identified as talented, they (and often others around them) tend to listen only to that moment. They may think, "This is it. There is no more." Their unselection places a ceiling over them. It's a false ceiling, but its effect is real.

The Glass Ceiling

Glass ceiling is a term introduced in 1978. Back then, it was a metaphor for the invisible, artificial obstacles that blocked women and "minorities" (which then meant people of color) from advancing

Recruitment Barriers and Promotions

The Glass Ceiling Commission pointed out that most organizations promote from within. Organizations not actively recruiting women had a smaller pool of women employees. As a result, the pool from which to promote women into upper management was also small. Basically, women got few chances to move up because there were so few women that they were often disregarded.

in their careers to management and executive positions. In 1991, Congress passed the Glass Ceiling Act, which established a commission to study how businesses and other organizations filled management and decision-making positions, trained people in the necessary qualifications for advancement into such positions, and used compensation programs and reward structures in the workplace.

The commission's findings showed that a glass ceiling did exist in the workplace (Glass Ceiling Commission 1995):

- Only 3 to 5 percent of senior management positions in Fortune 500 companies were held by women. Virtually all of these women were White.
- In places where women did hold senior positions, their compensation was lower than that of their male counterparts.
- In places where women held senior positions, they were in areas such as human resources, research, or other areas not usually on the career pathway to executive positions.

In addition, the commission found that women and minorities faced barriers to success as they tried to reach the upper echelons of management:

- prejudice and bias against women and people from "nonmainstream cultures"
- recruitment barriers
- lack of mentoring
- different performance evaluation standards for women and men

This situation sounds a lot like talent development in kids. When we pick the more mature, higher-achieving kids and tell them the sky's the limit, give them lots of chances to develop, give them access to mentors, and set high standards, we remove barriers for these kids. Conversely, when we disregard the less mature, struggling kids, give them less access to opportunities and fewer mentors, and have lower standards, we place barriers in their way. We build glass ceilings.

All Kids Can Learn

When I was twenty-two years old, I worked for an education outreach program called the Office of Youth Preparation, housed at Arizona State University. Its mission was to maximize educational opportunities for kids. We helped prepare kids in the city's schools for standardized tests, created classroom resources for teachers in districts with limited budgets, and hosted after-school programs to reach kids who otherwise wouldn't have had access to them. Our staff training and our approach to serving kids and teachers resulted in the smashing of ceilings.

One simple principle governed our work: *all kids can learn.* We were often working in under-resourced schools with teachers exhausted from years of teaching struggling, traumatized kids with little support. Our goal was to ensure that the kids at the public schools had just as many expectations and opportunities to succeed as the local private school kids had. This approach yielded higher standardized test scores in the schools where we worked, as well as greater teacher satisfaction and student engagement.

Why not view every kid as capable of leading the proverbial (or literal) Fortune 500 company? Why not provide all kids access to amazing mentors, teachers, or coaches who believe kids can do what they dream of? And why not put self-fulfilling prophecy to good use?

This experience led me to advocate for smashing ceilings. Why not view every kid as capable of leading the proverbial (or literal) Fortune 500 company? Why not provide all kids access to amazing mentors, teachers, or coaches who believe kids can do what they dream of? And why not put self-fulfilling prophecy to good use? Let's set high expectations for all kids.

While researching for this book, I visited and interviewed a variety of places that develop talent in young people. One of these places was Red Bull Salzburg, a professional hockey and soccer organization in Austria that also runs a youth academy, where the focus is on developing kids ages thirteen to eighteen as humans as well as players.

The academy spares no expense in the development of young people. It offers a dormitory and a private education system. Its staff includes full-time nutritionists, sport psychologists, physical therapists, trainers, and coaches. Its progressive athletic curriculum provides opportunities for all students to maximize their abilities as players and people. The adults at the academy avoid placing ceilings on any of its students.

At the time of my visit, Jesse Marsch was the head coach of the Red Bull Salzburg soccer team and was intimately involved with its youth academy. He was eternally optimistic and upbeat, and this approach was evident throughout the organization. He approached every situation with hard work and a can-do attitude. When I chatted with Marsch, he told a story that epitomized the idea of smashing ceilings.

Marsch recounted a time when he was conducting interviews for a position in the club. During one interview, he walked around to a few of the training sessions with the candidate. He chatted about the club as well as some individual players as he saw them practicing. As he passed a player, he would point out the player's skills and say, "This kid will be the next (name of an elite pro player here) soon." He did this over and over. The interviewee eventually said, "You keep saying that these players will all be something special. That is impossible." Marsch replied that it *wasn't* impossible if adults approached every single player as if they might be the next big thing. "That is our job," he said.

TDZ2 **To-Do List**

To create a Talent Development Zone that helps kids smash ceilings, adults need to:

- show kids there are no limits with your words and actions
- find role models for kids
- expose kids to ideas and opportunities

Show Kids There Are No Limits with Your Words and Actions

Adults often say limiting things to kids without realizing it. For example, "We don't need to visit that college," or, "That section of the library is for fifth graders." We do this without malice, but it still limits kids' views about where they belong and where they might go.

In a groundbreaking study called Learning Without Limits conducted from 1999 to 2004, the education faculty at Cambridge University collaborated to explore the effects of ability labeling and ability-focused practices (Hart et al. 2004). In 2005, a second phase of this research explored what might be possible if an entire school staff committed to creating an environment free from limiting beliefs about students' abilities and futures. This study was carried out at Wroxham School in Hertfordshire, England. Alison Peacock, head teacher at Wroxham School, explains that the team worked to enable all kids to surprise themselves and the adults around them with what they could achieve in this environment. She describes a few simple things the school staff did to remove limits (Swann et al. 2012):

- offering choices within lessons
- letting children make more decisions about the level of challenge they attempt
- giving more feedback about learning rather than just grades
- encouraging inventiveness
- encouraging openness to new ideas
- encouraging persistent questioning
- empathizing with children
- giving kids a chance to experience emotional stability

This approach to learning without limits yielded some interesting results—namely, giving children a sense of control, building intrinsic motivation, and providing emotional stability. These outcomes help learning in the following ways:

- **Giving kids control** lets them explore their world at their own pace, experience natural consequences, and make sense of those consequences.
- **Building intrinsic motivation** helps kids develop their talents because they want to.
- **Providing emotional stability** means adults give emotional support, understand kids' feelings, and show empathy. This creates a stable environment where kids feel safe to learn and fail, free from harsh judgment.

Here are a few concrete to-dos to help you show kids there are no limits with your words and actions:

- Create an environment free from your beliefs about what kids can or can't do.
  - Encourage kids to try new things.
  - When kids fail, be empathetic and understanding.
  - Introduce the power of *yet*. When kids say, "I can't do it," ask them to say (and believe), "I can't do it *yet*."

- Give kids opportunities to have control over their surroundings and their learning by letting them explore their world at their own pace and manage failure in their own time.
- Provide an emotionally safe environment.
  - Provide positive corrective feedback when kids make mistakes.
  - Help kids understand their feelings and manage their feelings and behavior.
  - Show empathy as kids express their emotions.

- Inspire intrinsic motivation. (For more on this, see TDZ5.)

Find Role Models for Kids

Role models serve some important purposes for kids. Initially, a role model sparks a desire and provides an example of something a child wants to learn. A child may say, "I want to do that! I see X doing it. I am going to save a video of that on my phone and practice it so I can be like X." A role model is inspiring, can show the proper way of doing a skill, and can help kids persevere as they practice the skill.

As you look to find role models, it's important to help kids see themselves in their role models. This vision propels them past a glass ceiling. When kids see a role model who looks like them, they can imagine themselves doing what that person does, and they're encouraged to emulate the role model. For example, if a young Black businesswoman sees a Black female executive in her company, she may think, "She is like me. I can become an executive too."

> When kids see a role model who looks like them, they can imagine themselves doing what that person does, and they're encouraged to emulate the role model.

Research evidence supports this idea. In one foundational study, researchers explored ways that race- and gender-matched role models provide young people with a greater sense of the opportunities available to them in the world. A longitudinal study of seventh graders who had at least one race- and gender-matched role model at the beginning of the study found that after twenty-four months, these students performed better academically, reported more achievement-oriented goals, enjoyed achievement-relevant activities to a greater degree, thought more about their futures, and looked up to adults rather than peers more often than did students without a race- and gender-matched role model (Zirkel 2002).

Research evidence notwithstanding, it's hard to quantify just how much of an impact, say . . . Lindsey Vonn has on girls and skiing or Kamala Harris has on girls of color. But we do know a few things:

- People don't attempt to achieve something unless they believe it can be done.
- People are much more likely to try to do things if they've seen that someone like them can do it.
- We are all impacted by somebody. If that person is a game changer and resembles you somehow, then you have someone to emulate.

Here are a few concrete to-dos to help you find role models to show kids:

- Find those role models.
  - Look at the people around you and ask your children's coaches, teachers, or friends for suggestions.
  - Watch what kids watch. Sometimes kids find role models on their own, and it will help you to know about them.
- Challenge kids to discover information about their role models. They can hop on the internet or visit the library to find books, videos, articles, and television programs.
- Talk about role models often. Be specific about what kids might find valuable in their example.
- Reach out to role models. Social media makes many of these folks accessible, or at least followable. If kids are old enough for social media and have family permission, encourage them to follow their role models and even ask them questions. Consider vetting the social media accounts beforehand to confirm that these folks understand they are role models and take it seriously, behaving and interacting in ways that are generally admirable.

Expose Kids to Ideas and Opportunities

How can you dream of reaching a destination if you don't know that place exists? You can't. You need exposure to ideas and opportunities.

The Truman Show is a 1998 movie that illustrates this concept. It's about a man, Truman Burbank, who grew up on the set of a reality show. The show takes place inside a massive studio. The whole world—except Truman—knows it's a studio. Truman simply thinks it's his life, which plays out on an island city. Truman has been conditioned to not cross the water in fear for his life. The studio is enclosed beneath an enormous domed ceiling. Truman ultimately chooses to summon his courage, cross the water, and break through the ceiling—literally.

Truman is able to cross the water and break through the ceiling only because he gets exposed to ideas along the way. As Truman is living his best life, small things happen to him that cause him to pause and think about his world. For example, a few actors hired for the show secretly want Truman to break out of his studio. They plant clues in Truman's path, in the form of comments and reading material, to let Truman know a bigger world might exist. In addition, Truman stumbles upon clues on his own, such as a light falling from the sky, an odd radio frequency, and an elevator that leads to nowhere. The biggest catalyst for Truman's break-through is love. He remembers someone from his past who has been removed from the set, and he decides that he just has to see her.

We are all a bit like Truman. We all have boundaries that have been placed on us in life. Some of us get exposed to other ideas and opportunities, and we decide we want more of it. But some of us never have those new experiences, and therefore our ambitions are limited. Exposing kids to variety in art, music, athletics, travel, literature, food, and other cultural experiences can open their minds and open doors to the future.

Here are a few concrete to-dos to help you expose kids to ideas and opportunities:

- Show them new ideas and opportunities.
  - New ideas and opportunities can help kids stretch in their endeavors, such as introducing a new instrument for a musician or a new technique for a kid who loves to bake.
  - Expose kids to completely new ideas and opportunities; these may spark a new interest or help them look at their passions differently. For example, Apple cofounder Steve Jobs audited a college calligraphy class just for the fun of it. Later, he credited this class for Apple's beautiful typography (Rosoff 2016).

- Explain those new ideas and opportunities.
  - Often kids can make sense of new things on their own, but sometimes they may need help understanding them.
  - Providing context may spur kids on to smash any ceilings they encounter.

- Notice what kids like about new ideas and opportunities, and give them more.

TDZ3
PROVIDE OPPORTUNITIES FOR DEEP, DELIBERATE PRACTICE

It takes lots and lots of practice to get good at something. Depending on what you read, the magic amount of practice is ten years, ten thousand hours, ten thousand repetitions, or some other variation of the number ten. But these numbers aren't magical, and they aren't rules; they are just guesses. And quality is just as important as quantity. Doing something for a certain number of hours or repetitions doesn't mean you are automatically getting good at it.

But just how important is deliberate practice? Where did these numbers come from? What is deep practice? Does deep practice have to be in the same area over and over again? Or should we take a multidisciplinary approach in order to develop talent?

Understanding Practice
Deliberate Practice

Anders Ericsson, Swedish psychologist, first linked the concept of deliberate practice—practice that involves improving technique while receiving a steady stream of critical feedback to improve weaknesses—to mastery or improved performance. Ericsson and his colleagues conducted two important studies on deliberate practice, created a framework to explain its importance, and discussed the effects of constraints such as motivation, resources, and effort on performance (Ericsson, Krampe, and Tesch-Romer 1993).

> Talent requires deep, deliberate practice.

These studies suggest that genetic factors play a role in some activities (such as height in basketball and perfect pitch in music), but that the amount of deliberate practice determines the impact of such innate gifts. It isn't enough just to show up with these gifts or just show up to practice. The "talented" still have to work to improve.

The research report goes on to say that chess masters and expert writers, scientists, mathematicians, swimmers, and other high-level performers all put in at least ten years of experience before they accomplished anything of note. Further, high-level performance by experienced people doesn't happen automatically. It develops as a result of deep, deliberate practice over time. In other words: the key isn't just time on task, it's *deliberate time on task*. "Many characteristics once believed to reflect innate talent are actually the result of intense practice extended for a minimum of 10 years" (Ericsson, Krampe, and Tesch-Romer 1993, 363).

Ericsson and colleagues name the hallmarks of deliberate practice: high-quality motivation, some instruction, feedback (mostly immediate), and teachers and coaches creating deliberate practice activities different from a person's normal play, work, or other activities. These designed deliberate activities do not replace one's "regular" play or work in a domain but rather supplement their other activities. In addition, they say some factors are essential in the realization of exceptional performance:

- **resources:** family interaction, coaching, and other opportunities
- **effort:** work invested over an extended period of time to allow adaptation to increasingly difficult demands in a chosen domain
- **motivation:** the desire to do an activity and work at it

These are pretty important findings about the pursuit of talent. They show that you don't need to be born with innate gifts in a particular performance domain to be good at it. Rather, talent requires deep, deliberate practice that happens outside one's normal activities and includes motivation, instruction, and feedback from a parent, teacher, mentor, or coach.

In *Peak: Secrets from the New Science of Expertise*, Ericsson and Robert Pool (2016) seek to clarify some misconceptions about talent development. They note that the practice rule of ten (ten years, ten thousand hours, ten thousand repetitions, or the like) is attractive because it's easy to remember and appealing because it fulfills a human desire to have a simple, concrete recipe for expertise. Then they go on to explain why the ten-thousand-hour rule (or a similar one) doesn't tell the whole story. There's nothing special or magical about ten thousand hours, they say; it's an average. In one part of his earlier research, Ericsson had simply chosen to refer to the total practice time a certain group of research subjects (violinists considered to be on track for international careers) had accumulated by the time they were twenty

> The amount of deliberate practice determines the impact of innate gifts.

years old. He and his colleagues estimated how many hours these violinists had spent working independently on improving their performance. They came up with an average of ten thousand hours. Malcolm Gladwell misinterpreted this figure, popularizing the "ten-thousand-hour rule" in his book *Outliers* (Wharton School 2016). Ericsson and Pool also note that the type of practice is just as important as the amount of practice. The ten-thousand-hour rule doesn't specify the type of practice. We shouldn't confuse activity with accomplishment.

Deep Practice

Daniel Coyle, author of *The Talent Code*, understood the value of the type of practice, and his book advocates for what he calls "deep practice." He says it takes multiple hours of this deep practice in a chosen field to get good at it. He describes deep practice as follows (Coyle 2009, 18):

- "operating at the edges of your ability, where you make mistakes"—which makes you smarter
- "struggling in certain targeted ways"

Remember Coyle's study on elite athletes discussed in chapter 2? He found that elite athletes accumulated more deliberate practice hours throughout their career than non-elite athletes did. Deep practice provides opportunities for success, failure, and improvement. So, improvement requires a bit of success and a bit of struggle. But why does making mistakes make you smarter? The mistakes that are bound to happen with deep practice strengthen neurological pathways—and we're back to brain plasticity. Our brains really are incredible organs.

So how do we engage in deep practice? Coyle suggests that we need to do three things:

- **Chunk it:** start with the whole and then break down the skill.
- **Repeat it:** practice, practice, practice with a focus on quality.
- **Feel it:** keep practicing until you feel the actions instead of actively thinking about them as you do them.

Practice Makes Myelin

Your brain is made up of neurons (nerve cells). Each neuron has three main parts: dendrites (which receive signals from other neurons), a cell body (which processes signals), and an axon (an extension that sends signals to other neurons). Myelin is a fatty substance that coats the axons, improving the speed and strength of bioelectrical signals. When you repeat an activity, the myelin coating on the participating neurons thickens, leading to a more efficient transfer of information. So, the more you practice deeply and deliberately, and the more you test your limits, the more myelination occurs, and the further you progress.

This description of deep practice is similar to the stages that people move through as they learn and master a motor skill:

- **The cognitive stage** (chunk it) is the beginning stage, when learners get a sense of the skill. They do a lot of visual learning and make a ton of mistakes.
- **The associative stage** (repeat it) is when learners practice repeatedly under varying circumstances with a focus on quality.
- **The automatic stage** (feel it) is when learners are doing the skill based on experience; it is now automatic. In this stage learners can feel the rightness or wrongness of their performance and can self-correct.

> Adults should try to nudge children gently to practice rather than forcing them.

Creating opportunities for deep, deliberate practice is key to helping kids develop their talents. But what do you do if kids don't want to deeply, deliberately practice? Maybe they have lost their passion for the activity. Maybe they are feeling pessimistic and unmotivated. Should you force them to practice?

Nope. Adults should try to nudge children gently to practice rather than forcing them. Nudging versus forcing is a question of timing, as well as the way in which we ask kids to practice. If we push too much, or push at a time when a child just really needs a break, we run the risk of the child pushing back and perhaps hating what they are doing. We want the child to *want* to practice.

Instead of asking a child why they aren't practicing, we might ask, "How can I support you? Are you having fun? What are your frustrations? How can I help?" And then we need to listen to the answers. Just like adults, sometimes kids simply want to be listened to. This may alleviate stress, provide comfort, and may even be reinvigorating.

What if kids want to pursue another area different from what they set out to practice? For example, what if a kid starts out as a soccer player and wants to play basketball? What if they start out playing the tuba and then want to play the drums? What if they play chess and want to write poetry? Can they still become talented?

Specialized Versus Multidisciplinary Practice

As we discussed in chapter 4, talent development is nonlinear. Sometimes the pursuit of talent means doing the same thing over and over again. Sometimes it involves changing the approach or domain entirely.

In the book *Range: Why Generalists Triumph in a Specialized World,* author David Epstein opens with an introduction titled "Roger vs. Tiger." Epstein was fascinated by how Roger Federer and Tiger Woods, both world-class athletes, ended up kings of their respective sports by taking radically different paths. Woods took a hyperspecialized path, focusing on golf exclusively from a very young age. Federer took a multidisciplinary approach, playing multiple sports with boundless energy before he decided to focus on tennis in his late teens.

To understand this, Epstein explores an idea proposed by psychologist Robin Hogarth: that some learning environments are "kind" and some are "wicked." Different endeavors require different types of practice (or learning environments) for skill development. Kind learning environments are ones in which predictable patterns occur and feedback is speedy and accurate—such as golf, chess, and classical music. In kind learning environments, a specialized practice approach works better. Wicked learning environments are ones without predictable patterns or quick, accurate feedback—such as tennis, soccer, school, and theater. In wicked learning environments, participants must constantly pivot, problem solve, and make choices.

Epstein argues then that most of life is a wicked environment and asserts that "the world is not golf, and most of it isn't even tennis. As Hogarth put it, much of the world is 'Martian tennis.' You can see the players on a court with balls and rackets, but nobody has shared the rules. It is up to you to derive them, and they are subject to change without notice" (Epstein 2019, 31). So he says that to prepare for life, and a lot of things in education, sports, or music, folks should be generalists instead of specialists.

He argues that in order to be really good in wicked environments, people are best served by gathering multiple experiences and perspectives on the problem. For example, if you want to be a good scriptwriter for a drama, you might want to sample comedy writing and horror writing to gain multiple unique perspectives and experiences, which might in turn help you write a richer, more thoughtful script. Or if you want to get good at soccer, perhaps you should sample tennis and basketball. Gaining experiences in adjacent wicked environments might prepare you for the unpredictable environment of soccer.

> When kids don't serendipitously bump into a good fit, they need adults to help them find it by providing experiences and opportunities.

In fact, sampling before specializing might be a good idea, as doing so helps you achieve "match quality"—a good fit between how a person is and what they do. Epstein isn't suggesting a casual once-over, but rather trial and error through sampling an activity, practicing it, thinking about whether you like it, and ultimately deciding whether to keep it up or move on. Sometimes match quality happens very early; for example, Wolfgang Amadeus Mozart found his fit with playing and composing music at age three. But sometimes it happens later in life; for example, Vincent Van Gogh didn't start painting in earnest until he was twenty-eight years old.

We briefly discussed this concept in chapter 4, which describes experience producing drive (EPD) theory. When kids don't serendipitously bump into a good fit, they need adults to help them find it by providing experiences and opportunities.

Here are a few key ideas to remember from Epstein's work:

- Kind learning environments require lots of deliberate practice.
- Wicked learning environments also require lots of deliberate practice, but perhaps in multiple areas, over time.
- Both learning environments require opportunities to engage in activities that match one's interests.
- Generalists and specialists both eventually specialize.

In the real-life examples in this chapter, individuals eventually put in a great deal of deep, deliberate practice in order to gain expertise. Each individual had an opportunity to pursue the sport, academic, music, or other area in which they eventually excelled.

Deep, Deliberate Practice and Talent Development

The concept of deep, deliberate practice is exactly what Françoys Gagné outlines in his Differentiated Model of Giftedness and Talent. Take another look at **the chart on page 28.** He doesn't use the word *practice*, but he's clearly talking about it in the "developmental process" section of the model. In this section, Gagné mentions activities, progress, and investment. Activities are what a person is doing. Investment is how much time and energy someone puts into the activity. Progress is a person's movement and change through the activities. *This is deep, deliberate practice.* If children *invest* time and energy into their *activities*, they have a great chance to *progress*.

TDZ3 **To-Do List**

To create a Talent Development Zone that helps kids get deep, deliberate practice, adults need to:

- employ Coyle's "chunk it, repeat it, feel it" approach
- help find or create enjoyable activities and challenges
- invest in the person
- ensure focused training instead of participation

Employ Coyle's "Chunk it, Repeat it, Feel it" Approach
Chunk It: Start with the Whole and Then Break Down the Skill

The idea here is to take a bigger skill, break it down into smaller parts, slowly master the parts, and then put the pieces back together—all with an eye to quality:

1. **Start with the whole.**
- Let kids play around and be creative with the skill.
- This allows kids to get comfortable with the skill on their own terms, which can build confidence and motivation—especially when done early, as part of the culture of the learning environment.
- Play and creativity also allow kids to break down the ideas of the skill on their own.

2. **Guide kids (or let kids guide themselves) to slow the skill down.**
- If you're guiding them:
   - o Ask them what they think is the best way to slow down the skill and break it into chunks.
   - o They will give a variety of answers depending on their age.
   - o Have some ideas in mind on how best to chunk the skill, and share them.

- If they're working independently:
  - o Make sure they have an idea of what the skill should look like when done correctly.
  - o Once they have an idea, the kids should break down that skill on their own in their head, write it down in chunks, or record it on video.
  - o The more detailed the breakdown is, the better.

Repeat It: Practice, Practice, Practice

Practice often, with an eye to getting better. The key is to ensure that the focus is on the quality—not the quantity—of the training. As children practice, they should be trying to get it right. Kids will make lots of mistakes, and that is a good thing. If children can't self-correct because they lack the knowledge or because they're frustrated or don't want to face their mistakes, then an adult should assist.

Feel It

The idea here is that once a person has chunked a skill and practiced it enough, then they can begin to feel the correctness of the skill. Have you ever done something and, after you did it, you said to yourself, "Wow, that felt good"? Or, when you are performing a skill in yoga or basketball or darts or guitar practice, you self-correct when it just doesn't feel right? That ability to feel the correctness of a skill says that you understand it inside your muscles and your mind.

This kinesthetic, intrinsic feedback can happen only if one puts sufficient high-quality time into a task through chunking and practicing phase. Reaching this stage does not mean that external feedback is no longer needed. In fact, as people get good at a skill and want to keep improving, they will need someone else to make it more difficult for them. Ratcheting up the pressure is a good thing, if the coach or teacher knows how to do it so the learner stays motivated and confident but also stretched, and if the learner has the coping skills to manage the pressure. (For more information on this, see the sections on motivation and confidence below under "Invest in the Person.")

Here are a few suggestions to help learners "feel it":

- **Build the learner's awareness of how the skill feels.** Start by asking how it feels.
- **Listen to the learner and provide feedback.** Listen intently, as learner-provided information is critical to giving constructive feedback.
- **Encourage kids to see if they can correct their own mistakes.** Give kids some ideas on what they can do to help themselves feel the skill. This enables them to program their self-talk as they move through their skill-building process.

Help Find or Create Enjoyable Activities and Challenges

Helping young people seeking to improve in taekwondo, chemistry, or bassoon is about providing access to activities that are engaging, challenging, and presented in a way that excites and motivates them:

- **Determine the domain and find some examples online.**
  - Ask a specialist to point you in the right direction.
  - Make sure activities cover content both for now and for later.
  - Make sure the activities are appropriately challenging.

- **Provide access to these activities.** Whether online or in person, the key is to make sure the developing child can actually do what you're suggesting.

Invest in the Person

Making an investment is devoting time, effort, or energy to a particular undertaking with the expectation of a worthwhile result. When it comes to kids and talent development, we are talking about two kinds of investment: the child's and the adult's.

The investment that the child is making is one of energy and high-quality time on task. Kids need to choose to make this investment on their own. When kids choose to do something as opposed to being told to do something, they are spending their own currency to get what they want, and it's more meaningful and effective.

It is on you—the coach, teacher, or parent—to create an environment that provides timely advice or ideas on how the child can make savvy investments. As you help them along, they will gain greater understanding, motivation, and confidence and in time will be able to make their own investment choices and strategies.

Ensure Focused Training Instead of Participation

If kids want to improve their skills, they must focus on the quality of the tasks they are doing as opposed to simply the quantity of time they are putting into the endeavor:

- **Don't confuse activity with accomplishment.**
  - Kids should understand that just because they put in time doesn't mean they will improve.
  - Kids should have an idea of what they want to improve and how they want to improve it and move toward that idea deliberately.
  - Kids can write it down. Sometimes writing down goals makes them easier to shoot for—and hold themselves accountable to.

- **Focus on quality versus quantity.**
  - The goal for kids should be on the feel and the details of the skill, not simply putting in a certain amount of time or repetitions.
  - If kids make mistakes, don't worry. It's effort toward quality—not perfection—that counts.

- **Ensure opportunities for other endeavors if kids want them, and offer breaks if they don't.**
  - Provide opportunities for other activities, subjects, or sports.
  - Provide opportunities for breaks.
  - Give kids reasons and real-life examples as to why variety and breaks are a good idea.

I have three sons who want to play soccer all the time and do not want to play another organized sport. But we don't go full-throttle on soccer year-round, because I know the perils of early specialization and lack of preparation for the wicked learning environment of the real world. So we build in opportunities for different experiences.

Over the course of a year we provide variety and breaks to ensure growth, maturation, and mental recharging. We encourage our sons to surf, skateboard, or play basketball with friends. We provide opportunities to grow mentally by reading about various athletes or watching films about successful people in multiple domains. Also, we enforce no-soccer intervals. We give the boys different balls, sports equipment, and other gear to play with during these times.

Often one or more of the boys balks at the suggestion of another sport or activity. When this happens, we reason through our suggestion and explain to them the benefits. They usually come around and end up enjoying the break from soccer. And when they come back to their favorite sport, they feel rejuvenated and excited—and carrying some wicked experience to add to their skill set.

TDZ4
BUILD REALISTIC OPTIMISM

Optimism is hopefulness and confidence about the future or about a successful outcome. When facing a difficult moment, an optimist will see an opportunity, whereas a pessimist will see a problem. An optimistic attitude has propelled many a person into persisting at a task in order to improve, get an A on an exam, or win a game.

"The pessimist complains about the wind; the optimist expects it to change; the realist adjusts the sails."

I am an advocate of a particular kind of optimism: realistic optimism. Realistic optimism is a clear-eyed, positive attitude. Realistic optimists understand that no amount of positivity will help them if what they are doing is ineffective. They know they may need to make some adjustments in their efforts. A quote by motivational writer William Arthur Ward perfectly explains realistic optimism: "The pessimist complains about the wind; the optimist expects it to change; the realist adjusts the sails."

Understanding Optimism

We can all probably agree that an optimistic outlook is better than a pessimistic outlook. Optimism is correlated with many positive outcomes, including increased life expectancy, better general health, better mental health, more success in sports and work, and better coping strategies in the face of adversity. What is more: the way we explain obstacles and failure influences our next steps. An optimistic explanatory style stops helplessness, while a pessimistic explanatory style spreads helplessness.

So, when kids fail or get bad news, teachers, coaches, and parents can help them view next steps with an optimistic *I can do this* approach. This approach will give kids a leg up in their pursuits. But what if a kid just keeps doing the same things over and over with a positive attitude? Is this going to help them improve?

Too Much of a Good Thing

How can a lot of a good thing be bad? Let's look at some examples.

- **Excessive optimism with money:** What if someone had invested in a stock, and it wasn't doing well? A pure optimist, or what some would call an extreme optimist, might stick with the investment. They might choose to ignore signs or advice that they need to change course. And in the end, they might lose a lot of money as a result.

- **Excessive optimism in health:** There is a lot of research evidence showing that optimism can improve your physical and mental health (Rasmussen, Scheier, and Greenhouse 2010; Conversano et al. 2010). But what if you are an optimist and believe that you are healthy despite signs to the contrary and risk factors in your family history? This kind of optimism could lead you to ignore facts that, when viewed objectively, could lead to important—even life-saving—changes in your behavior and medical care.

- **Excessive optimism in marriage:** Ask newlywed couples about their chances of divorce, and you will get almost universally optimistic answers. But the truth is that that about 40 percent of marriages in the United States end in divorce (Luscombe 2018). Optimism about marriage isn't a bad thing, but marriage takes work in addition to optimism. Optimistic marriage partners should also ensure that they are being realistic and working to change or improve things as needed.

Extreme optimists, or blind optimists (coaches, teachers, parents, and children included), may have too much faith in the future and as a result may not work as hard to create a different approach or plan B when plan A isn't succeeding. They may look only at the positive side of situations, ignoring uncomfortable occurrences or critiques. They may do this because they lack coping skills and find it easier to just look at the bright side.

Children and those who work with children will always face hurdles as they strive to develop talent. They must be confident and optimistic, certainly. But they must also be willing and able to adapt when things aren't going well.

Realistic Optimism

Sophia Chou is an organizational psychology researcher at National Taiwan University. She uses the phrase *realistic optimists* to describe folks who combine the positive attitude of optimists with the clear-sighted view of pessimists. Chou worked in business for several years and noticed that some folks combined optimism with realism and tended to succeed. She wondered whether the seemingly contradictory ideas of realism and optimism were actually intertwined (Ghose 2013).

Chou conducted a study in which she administered personality surveys to more than two hundred college students in Taiwan. The surveys tested how many "positive illusions" the students held, as well as whether they were motivated more by reality or by self-enhancement (maintaining self-esteem). She found:

- Realistic optimists tended to choose accuracy over self-enhancement, whereas unrealistic optimists tended to choose self-enhancement.

- Realistic optimists got better grades, on average, than their peers (probably because they didn't fool themselves into thinking they would do well without working hard or studying).

- Realistic optimists managed to be happy (partly because they believed they had more control over their interpersonal relationships, as well as self-control). Chou said, "Every time they face an issue or a challenge or a problem, they won't say 'I have no choice and this is the only thing I can do.' They will be creative, they will have a plan A, plan B and plan C" (Ghose 2013).

We can surmise from this research that if we take a realistic approach to our endeavors, we will likely want to pursue getting it right. We'll work harder to seek better performance. We'll be happier as a result of having some control, and we'll be willing to have and implement alternative plans. It's easy to see how this approach might be valuable for talent seekers and talent developers.

Let's play out a typical youth scenario. A young athlete has made several errors and is aware of them. This kid is an optimist and believes the result can be altered with effort. This belief is steadfast. Eventually the child's team loses the game, and this kid played a role in the loss. Their effort, attitude, and belief remained fantastic, but they didn't make the changes needed to ensure success. Though this kid is an optimist, being an optimist doesn't necessarily mean that the person is willing to change their actions. It just means that they have a fantastic attitude. Attitude is important, but it's not the only ingredient needed for improvement and success.

> Attitude is important, but it's not the only ingredient needed for improvement and success.

Now let's think about this more generally. Let's say the athlete above gets cut from the team. Or suppose we're talking about academics, and an optimistic child does not make it into a gifted and talented program. Is the kid willing to stay optimistic but also be realistic and change directions as needed? Believing and not changing may feel good, because it protects self-esteem. But this approach isn't enough in the pursuit of talent. Sometimes kids have to adjust the sails.

The bottom line is that optimism is better than pessimism. Pessimistic people are more anxious, more likely to follow up a bad performance with another one, and likely to have less motivation overall. But too often we take a black-and-white view, as if people are *either* optimistic *or* pessimistic. People can have optimism with a dose of realism.

I strongly advocate being optimistic in the face of adversity. I do think it is critical to stay *positive* in the moment and to look at all situations as manageable. But I also think realism is critical. It is important to continually examine what needs changing from moment to moment and day to day. I advocate that children and those who work with children be *positive* in terms of *moving forward* to find solutions. Success in education, sports, or the arts depends on one's ability to navigate treacherous waters and be willing change course when necessary. Children should learn that there will be moments when they may make a mistake, have a bad moment, or get critical feedback. Let's teach them how to maintain optimism under pressure but also to be ready to adapt to meet the demands of the situation.

TDZ4 **To-Do List**

To create a Talent Development Zone that helps kids build realistic optimism, adults need to:

- maintain optimism
- help kids be self-aware
- help kids manage and direct their self-talk

Maintain Optimism

Helping children maintain an optimistic outlook is critical. Kids often face moments that can define their talent development journey. They need to keep their focus on what they *can* do to change versus what they *can't* do. Here are a few simple ways you can help kids remember this:

- **Remind them what they can do.** Chat with kids often as they engage in their activities. Tell them that while they may not be good at everything, they are good at some things. This reminds them that they are winning small successes on their way to reaching their big goals.
- **Keep them excited about reaching.** Tell kids that the best fruit is at the end of the branch and that reaching for it is a good thing. The excitement of reaching will keep them passionate and engaged as they seek to improve their skills.
- **Don't dwell on the past.** Sometimes dwelling feels good, but it isn't productive. Remind kids that setbacks happen, and encourage them to keep going. Perhaps allow them to feel the pain and talk about it, but then say, "Okay, it is what it is. Let's reach for the next step."
- **Be positive.** For kids who are trying hard, having you in their corner cheering them on is important. As you provide constructive criticism, end with positive comments.

Help Kids Be Self-Aware

In order to develop realistic optimism, we must be truly aware of what is going on. Sometimes, in the interest of emotional self-preservation, we don't acknowledge our mistakes. Mistakes happen, and that is okay. But making progress in the real world requires awareness of missteps and the ability to change course. Here are a few simple ways you can help kids be more self-aware:

- **Teach kids to be honest with themselves.** Sometimes kids protect themselves because it hurts to admit mistakes. Sometimes they are perfectionists and don't give themselves credit when credit is due. Help them learn how to be honest with themselves by providing honest and objective feedback. Take video or audio recordings or show kids examples of work that's like theirs.

- **Teach kids that it's okay to be honest with themselves.** Being honest with themselves means putting their pride on the line. This is not easy for anyone, so consistently tell and show children it's okay to be wrong—or right. Reality is what it is, and it's best to acknowledge it.

- **Be a role model.** Showing others how to be self-aware sometimes means calling out your own behavior in front of others. Admit your mistakes in front of kids. Talk about what you did well or poorly. Describe your feelings about your performance. Talk about how you might change your approach going forward.

Help Kids Manage and Direct Their Self-Talk

Everybody has a running internal dialogue. In big moments, this self-talk can turn negative and get the better of a person. Here are a few simple ways you can help kids direct their self-talk to their advantage instead:

- **Help kids program their self-talk by setting a good example.** Be mindful of what you say, because as poet Daniel Ladinsky wrote, "What we speak becomes the house we live in." What you say sticks with kids, and in many cases is what they repeat over and over to themselves.

- **Help kids recognize what they are saying and when they are saying it.** Kids can learn to be aware of their self-talk in big moments. Ask them questions after events, or give them a heads-up to pay attention to their self-talk. Suggest that they take notes afterward and look at them later to assess if they were feeling optimistic, realistic, pessimistic, or a combination.

- **Tell kids that they can change their self-talk.**

  o Remind kids that what they say to themselves is their choice and can be changed, but it takes work.

  o Have kids try to:

    · recognize when they are saying things to themselves and what they are saying

    · picture a stop sign in their head if their self-talk is negative

    · replace negative statements with some go-to optimistic but realistic statements (see below)

- **Have kids write down some optimistic but realistic go-to statements.** These statements might include things like *Keep after it*; *I can do it*; *I can get there*; *Okay, I can change this*; or *That wasn't quite right, but I can try it differently the next time*. Practice these statements daily. Challenge kids to use them in their daily lives.

TDZ5
FOSTER IN KIDS A LOVE FOR THEIR ENDEAVORS

Do you like your work? My guess is some of you do, some don't, and others lie somewhere in between. But does it matter? Does your fondness for your work affect your performance, creativity, long-term happiness, and persistence?

The word *work* triggers a variety of reactions in people. Some folks cringe because they hate working out or doing housework, paperwork, and the like. Some loathe their job and show up every day simply to collect a paycheck or because the job needs doing. They do the work because they have to, not because they want to.

Some folks are excited when they hear the word *work*. They love going to their jobs or exercising or doing other tasks every day, and thinking about it invigorates them. They do the work because they want to, not because they have to.

And many people land somewhere in the middle. You may have heard the adage *find a job you love and you will never work a day in your life.* This means if you do something you love for work, it won't seem tedious, mind numbing, or soul sucking. You won't feel as if your job takes you away from something you love. You may feel

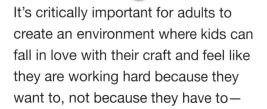

It's critically important for adults to create an environment where kids can fall in love with their craft and feel like they are working hard because they want to, not because they have to— where kids are intrinsically motivated.

lucky that you get to make money at your job. If this sounds like you, you know that it is a wonderful thing to show up for work and truly enjoy being there. You also know that even at a job you love, some days are a grind.

You are human, and sometimes even the most enjoyable work is difficult, and even fabulous jobs likely entail at least a few tasks you'd simply rather ignore. However, if you are doing something you love, there will probably be more good days than bad. Your feelings about your work can have a profound effect on how well, how long, how passionately, and how creatively you do your work—both when things are easy and when they're stressful.

Kids are no different from adults in this regard. To maximize their talent development, they need to love what they do. Kids can even learn to enjoy the difficult moments in pursuit of that which they love. When kids are engaged in deep, deliberate practice, that process will not be smooth sailing every day. Sometimes their endeavors require copious amounts of hard work. It's critically important for adults to create an environment where kids can fall in love with their craft and feel like they are working hard because they want to, not because they have to—where kids are intrinsically motivated.

Understanding Intrinsic Motivation

Motivation is a force, stimulus, or influence that energizes, sustains, and directs human behavior. The two key components of motivation are direction and intensity. Direction refers to what you are trying to accomplish, while intensity refers to the effort you put into the pursuit. Evidence suggests that enhanced motivation improves performance, strengthens learning, promotes enjoyment, and increases persistence in performance settings (Wilson 2006). So, how can we enhance motivation? And what kind of motivation should we enhance?

Here is a story that illustrates the two main types of motivation—intrinsic and extrinsic (Wilson 2006):

> There was a man who lived in a house that had a lawn. Every day children would come to play different sports in his large yard. The man started to be annoyed by this activity and decided to change it. So, one day he went to the kids and paid them a dollar to come play on his lawn. Well, of course the kids were thrilled by this bit of good fortune and were happy to oblige. The next day the kids showed up again, but this time the man only gave them fifty cents. On the third day when the kids showed up, the man told them that he didn't have any money left, but that they were welcome to come play in his yard. The kids were not happy. They said, "Forget this! We aren't playing here anymore," and left the yard.

The kids were initially intrinsically motivated to play in the man's yard. Through rewards, they became extrinsically motivated over time. Then, when pressed to play in the yard without extrinsic rewards, they quit.

Research shows that when people engage in tasks because they want to (they're intrinsically motivated) as opposed to doing tasks because they have to (they're extrinsically motivated), they enjoy the work more, perform better under pressure, show more creativity, and persist in the face of difficulty. Let's take a look at a few studies and discussions of intrinsic motivation in education, youth sports, and other domains.

In Education

Intrinsic motivation is powerful in the pursuit of academic improvement and important for kids in school. Intrinsic motivation in education is measured using the following criteria:

- how well the learner could persist at an assigned task
- how much time the learner spent trying the task
- how much innate curiosity the student used

- how much confidence the student had relative to an activity
- how big a desire the student had to select an activity

A student who is intrinsically motivated will persist at a given task, even if it is difficult, with no need for a reward. This type of student is more likely to finish the task and be enthusiastic about difficult activities. Finally, students who are intrinsically motivated are more likely to learn the information and to feel confident about trying new learning environments.

> Students who are intrinsically motivated are more likely to learn the information and to feel confident about trying new learning environments.

This is not to say that extrinsic motivation is always bad—it's not. But the research in this area shows that extrinsic motivation may interfere with intrinsic motivation, as in the story on page 70. In creative forms of work and learning, it may be better not to offer rewards for completing tasks; this may negatively influence a child's overall motivational orientation.

Take all of this together, and we can see that:

- Intrinsic motivation is key for kids tackling new things, doing things for a long period of time, pursuing difficult tasks, and being creative.
- Extrinsic motivation can hinder creativity.
- Adults can have an influence on children's intrinsic motivation.

In Youth Sports

Hundreds of youth sports studies over the years have produced similar findings. In research ranging from competitive swimmers to high-level youth soccer players and from children in physical education classes to young college athletes, the results are remarkably consistent. Athletes who showed more self-determination (intrinsic motivation) enjoyed their sport more, persisted when the activity got more difficult, felt less negative stress, and were more creative in their pursuits (Fenton, Duda, and Barrett 2016).

Competence, Autonomy, and Relatedness

Why does this happen? And more importantly, how can adults impact kids' motivation to reap these benefits of intrinsic motivation? The environment that surrounds a child influences their motivation. This environment is created by the behaviors of others—namely teachers, coaches, parents, and so on. Adults, and the environment that they create, help kids learn to be more intrinsically motivated by focusing on three innate needs: competence, autonomy, and relatedness. When these innate needs are met regarding a particular activity, intrinsic motivation increases and people are more likely to engage in the activity because they want to (rather than because they have to). When these innate needs are not met, motivation is more likely to be extrinsic, and people are more likely to disengage, be unable to handle pressure, and quit when things get difficult.

> 66
>
> Adults, and the environment that they create, help kids learn to be more intrinsically motivated by focusing on three innate needs: competence, autonomy, and relatedness.

Competence

Competence is feeling that you understand and are good at an activity. If an adult wants to improve a kid's intrinsic motivation for an activity, the goal as related to competence is to ensure that the kid feels that they are good at, or getting good at, whatever they are doing. Think about it. How motivated are you to engage in an activity if you feel you are good at it or getting better at it? (You're likely very motivated.) But how likely are you to engage in an activity if you feel you aren't good at it and have no chance at getting better? (You're likely unmotivated.)

Creating an environment that improves a child's perception of how good they are at something they're doing will improve their intrinsic motivation. This perception is built on conversations and practice sessions over time, during which the child learns what it means to be competent (and can judge their own skill accurately and honestly) and the adult learns to communicate effectively with the child at appropriate times about their progress.

Autonomy

Autonomy is how much choice you feel you have with regard to a task. When children feel that they have some choice in what they are doing (what, when, how long, and so forth), they also feel more in control. Having some choice in an endeavor is likely to improve intrinsic motivation. But what sorts of choices should adults offer children, and how much choice is appropriate?

There's no single answer to the question of how much choice to offer. But if we give children opportunities for choice within their required play, learning, study, practice, competition, or performance times in academics, sports, and the arts, this will increase their intrinsic motivation. In addition, if we give children opportunities to have extra child-led play times (mess around with their instrument, read for pleasure, engage in problem-solving projects away from school, kick the ball against the wall at the park with friends, and so on) and they choose to do it, that is a good thing. The more these times occur, the more intrinsic motivation there is, and the more opportunity kids will have to incur all the benefits of intrinsic motivation.

Give kids some freedom in their tasks and activities. Be creative in fitting children's choices into your master plan. This choice has a major impact on their internal desire to participate and perform.

Relatedness

Relatedness usually refers to how connected a child feels to a group they are involved with in the classroom, the arts, or sports. But relatedness can also mean the child feels connected to you, an adult in charge—they feel that you are on their team, in their corner, and part of their quest to develop their talent. If a child feels they are part of a group, then their intrinsic motivation is likely to increase.

Kids deserve to have an environment that satisfies their three innate needs so they can be intrinsically motivated. Doing things because they *want* to, not because they *have* to, allows kids to improve, persist, enjoy, and create as they develop their talents.

TDZ5 **To-Do List**

To create a Talent Development Zone that fosters in kids a love for their endeavors through intrinsic motivation, adults need to:

- build competence
- provide choice (autonomy)
- ensure group cohesion (relatedness)

Build Competence
Set Self-Referenced Success Criteria
When kids put themselves out there as you are asking them to, at some point they will struggle to hit a target. If you tell them over and over, "This is how we define success; look at how you are improving; if you aren't satisfied, how can you work to improve?" you can help them feel competent at the task. Feeling competent sometimes involves failures—and that's okay.

Call Attention to Data That Show Improvement
Use evidence to help kids develop a gradual sense of how good they are getting. This slow processing and realizing they are improving is a great motivator. It is the number one way to build confidence as well.

Provide Choice (Autonomy)
Ask Instead of Tell
When kids are practicing a skill, if you ask them what the right thing to do is (instead of telling them what to do), this gives them a chance to think things through and choose an answer for themselves. When kids are able to choose an answer or an option, it's very motivating.

Create Perception of Choice
Sometimes the perception of choice is all kids need. Give them some freedom in their activities. Be creative in fitting kids' choices into your master plan. Choice has a major impact on kids' internal desire to participate and perform.

Ensure Group Cohesion (Relatedness)

Are you building a strong, cohesive group by ensuring that each individual feels a sense of belonging? A group can take many forms, such as a class, team, orchestra, cast of a play, a duo or trio, or even an individual (with you as the rest of the "group"). Group cohesion is powerful. How many times have you seen a weaker team roll through a championship because of its strong bond? Sometimes group members take it upon themselves to build this bond, but often it is the adult in charge who establishes an environment where individuals feel welcome and valued. For detailed information on building a cohesive group culture, see TDZ10.

TDZ6
DEVELOP AND INSPIRE CREATIVITY

Creativity is the ability to see new opportunities, to produce original ideas, to adapt to changing situations, and to apply imagination to solve complex problems. What is the role of creativity in helping kids develop their talents?

Understanding the Role of Creativity

Your mission as an adult is to help each child find a way to develop their talent however they can. You do this by offering new opportunities and original ideas and by being flexible.

Kids might be highly motivated and optimistic and practice really hard, but when they hit a roadblock in the pursuit of talent, often a good attitude and lots of effort isn't quite enough. The roadblock isn't simple, so the way around it isn't simple either. It requires a creative approach. Consider Thomas Edison's work. He conducted more than ten thousand experiments with various chemicals and materials while developing a nickel-iron automotive battery. He kept after it creatively over many years. When a friend lamented the time and money Edison had spent with no results, Edison fired back, "Results! Why, man, I have gotten a lot of results! I know several thousand things that won't work" (Dyer and Martin 1910).

The Candle Problem

The candle problem was designed in 1945 by psychologist Karl Duncker. In it he gave participants a small candle, a box of thumbtacks, and a book of matches and asked them to determine how best to affix the candle to the wall (Duncker 1945). The ideal solution is to empty the thumbtacks from the box, tack the box to the wall, then tack the candle to the box.

Daniel Pink gave a TED Talk in 2009 describing how researchers all over the world have replicated this study with different twists. For example, scientists Sam Glucksberg and Robert Weisberg conducted a version of the study to measure the influence of extrinsic versus intrinsic motivation on task performance (Glucksberg and Weisberg 1966). In this study, the participants were timed. Glucksberg and Weisberg told some of them the timing was simply to find out how long, on average, it takes people to solve the problem. They told other participants that if they were in the fastest 25 percent, they'd get monetary rewards. The latter participants did consistently worse than the former.

Pink noted that the people who were offered money performed slower because they were feeling stress. This stress hindered their problem-solving, and the promise of rewards dulled their thinking and blocked their creativity. Rewards narrow people's focus. This effect is helpful when the goal is clear and simple, requiring plain hard work. But when the goal requires creativity, rewards do more harm than good.

We are all facing versions of the candle problem every day. For kids trying to develop their talents, solutions to obstacles they encounter are often not obvious and require a methodical, *creative* approach. To help kids along, adults can create an environment that fosters intrinsic motivation and a love of what they do. "The secret to high performance isn't rewards and punishments, but . . . the drive to do things because they matter" (Pink 2009).

We already know from TDZ5 that satisfying a child's three innate needs (competence, autonomy, and relatedness) fosters intrinsic motivation. Satisfying these needs allows a child the necessary mental freedom to pursue a solution that isn't obvious.

Incongruence

In TDZ3 we discussed David Epstein's concept of range—specialization versus a multidisciplinary approach—and its effect on talent development. In his book *Range*, Epstein also discusses the importance of incongruence and congruence (Epstein 2019). Congruence is a social science term that describes when the elements of an organization's culture (values, goals, leadership styles, and so on) all point in the same direction, reinforcing one another and promoting consistency and efficiency. Incongruence, then, is when the elements don't necessarily fit together—when people are thinking or acting outside the box.

Through real-life stories, Epstein illustrates how thinking outside the box might happen within an organization and why it might be important. Epstein uses an example from NASA, where, as in many organizations, people tend to go by the book, or follow procedure—sometimes to a fault. Experienced professionals are used to being successful by doing what has worked in the past. Epstein calls this "overlearned behavior." But sometimes, "we have always done it this way" can be counterproductive. Tragically, this overlearned behavior resulted in the *Challenger* explosion on January 28, 1986, when the O-ring rubber seals in the joints of the rocket boosters failed in the cold temperatures on launch day. The team had not analyzed O-ring data in an outside-the-box way that would have allowed a decision not to launch the shuttle.

The NASA environment on the day of the launch was a wicked one. (For more on wicked environments, see page 56.) In other words, it was unpredictable and required the ability to pivot, problem solve, and make choices. Wicked environments need a creative approach. This, in turn, takes a bit of incongruence.

Epstein says that an effective problem-solving culture is one that balances standard practice with ideas and solutions that push against standard practice. He says that if members of a group are used to group cohesion, encouraging distinctiveness or individuality helps them show what he calls "ambidextrous thought" and adapt to varied situations. Conversely, if mem-

> Tell kids: don't just follow the rules because they're rules—look for solutions because there's a problem that needs solving.

bers of a group are used to working alone, then having them work together sometimes helps the problem-solving process. He suggests expanding a group's range by identifying the group's cultural norms and tweaking them in another direction to help change perspectives and hopefully foster problem-solving.

So, what can we learn from this? How can incongruence inspire creativity and help kids develop their talents?

Being creative is looking for a solution where there isn't an obvious one. While kids do this sometimes, other times they keep doing the same thing over and over because the rules say they should do it this way and it has worked before. But eventually, it doesn't work. Now what? Can they take an unconventional approach?

When you establish incongruence in your learning environment, kids will be inspired to be creative when something that usually has worked does not work. Balance the idea of using data with *also* looking outside the data. Tell kids: don't just follow the rules because they're rules— look for solutions because there's a problem that needs solving. In other words, inspire creative problem-solving.

Creative Problem-Solving in Sports

Creativity in sports can be fun to watch. For example, in a basketball game, a chest pass, a dribble, or a feint of the hips may be an unscripted, in-the-moment, outside-the-rulebook solution to get by a defender or make a basket. When athletes get creative, they're reading situations instead of rules.

In 2019 I visited TOVO Academy Barcelona, a soccer academy in Spain that trains young players to be creative as they pursue their talent. TOVO's methodology is meant to develop "players of great cognition, competence, and character." It encourages players to "seek effective solutions with vision, precision, and pace" (TOVO Institute, n.d.). This training is a unique way of teaching kids to be creative as they look for solutions in the game.

TOVO was created and is run by Todd Beane. Beane is the son-in-law of Johan Cruyff, a legendary Dutch soccer player and coach who changed the way people saw and taught soccer in the 1980s and 1990s. Cruyff was a player at Ajax (a team in the Netherlands professional league) and Barcelona (a team in Spain) and was famous for being an incredibly smart and creative soccer player and coach. Here are a few of his quotes, which illustrate his approach to the game (Guardian Sport 2016; Keel 2016):

- "What is speed? The sports press often confuses speed with insight. See, if I start running slightly earlier than someone else, I seem faster."

- "You play football with your head, and your legs are there to help you."

- "I find it terrible when talents are rejected based on computer stats. Based on the criteria at Ajax now I would have been rejected. When I was 15, I couldn't kick a ball 15 meters with my left and maybe 20 with my right. My qualities, technique, and vision are not detectable by a computer."

These quotes show that Cruyff believed soccer is a game of the mind, and it's all about problem-solving. This was the idea behind his methodology as a player and coach. His son-in-law Beane has created a place for kids to develop their talent in an environment rich with opportunities for problem-solving and creativity.

TOVO is a live-in training facility that provides a holistic soccer and life education. Kids of all ability levels, genders, and cultures come there from all over the world. TOVO staff teach the principles of cognition, competition, and character—the three Cs—throughout every training in a scoped and sequenced way. But it isn't just *what* is being taught; it is also *how* it is being taught that inspires and rewards creativity.

When I interviewed Beane during my visit, he explained, "We have developed a detailed rubric that defines the complete footballer a young player must become if he is to maximize his potential. . . . We begin to analyze and train every aspect of performance. An intelligent player capable of executing his options in real time under real pressure is a player that will be prepared to compete at a higher level."

Beane described cognition as how kids make sense of their environment. The environment, in this case, is the soccer field in various training exercises and activities. He avoids drills, which he describes as rote and structured. Instead, TOVO creates activities in which players can solve problems and create.

Cognition training consists of six steps: perceive, conceive, decide, deceive, execute, and assess. To *perceive* means to make meaning of available information. Does the player have the ball or not? What is the problem that needs solving? This starts the process of creativity. To *conceive* means to think of a way to solve the problem at hand—for example, by dribbling or passing in a variety of directions and speeds. Coaches do not tell the players what to do; rather, they guide players through a discovery process by asking a series of questions leading toward possible solutions. In addition, coaches teach players to scan the area before they receive the ball so they have choices in mind prior to receiving the ball and can exploit space and execute their choices successfully once they have the ball. Players then *decide* and *deceive* as they *execute* their choice. (*Decide and deceive* is an "invasion sports" idea. Some examples of invasion sports are basketball, hockey, soccer, lacrosse, rugby, and football. Whenever you encounter a player, you have to make a decision, then fool your opponent, then execute your decision to get around the opponent.) Finally, they *assess* how their choice played out.

Of course, a lot of failure happens during this process. Failure is encouraged, not reprimanded. The TOVO staff understand that development is a journey, and it takes time. The idea is to move from panic to poise and purpose, then to proficiency. In our 2019 conversation, Beane said over and over that "true creativity is the vision, not the skill" and that "sulking or celebrating a result isn't great as the player would be living in the past and true creativity necessitates the player be in the moment and prepare for the future."

The six-step cognition process builds confidence and competence over time, through high-quality repetitions. Competence, in this case, means fitness and the effective execution of techniques.

Finally, Beane said that the development of character in players is very important at TOVO. He described character in players as having ambition, respect, and resilience. Developing and rewarding these characteristics allows athletes to carry out the cognition required in the TOVO approach.

Creative Problem-Solving in Education

Creative problem-solving (CPS) is a method often used in education. It's a process that helps kids redefine problems and opportunities they might face; come up with unique, imaginative, innovative responses and solutions; and then take action. The CPS process was developed by Alex Osborn in the 1940s and then improved upon in collaboration with Sidney J. Parnes and Ruth Noller in the 1950s in ways that are still used today.

In his 1953 book *Applied Imagination*, Osborn describes two distinct kinds of thinking: divergent and convergent thinking. *Divergent thinking* is the process of generating potential solutions and

Use a balanced combination of divergent and convergent thinking to develop new ideas or solutions. If there's not enough divergent thinking, idea generation may be stifled. If there's not enough convergent thinking, decisions may not be fully thought out.

possibilities for a problem or situation. This process is sometimes called brainstorming. *Convergent thinking* is the process of evaluating the options and choosing the one (or ones) that best fits the needs of the situation. People use a combination of divergent and convergent thinking to develop new ideas or solutions. Balanced use of both kinds of thinking is important. If there's not enough divergent thinking, idea generation may be stifled. If there's not enough convergent thinking, decisions may not be fully thought out.

The CPS model has been used a lot in classrooms (and boardrooms) over the decades. As a result, researchers have extensively studied its effectiveness in fostering creativity to arrive at a solution. As Scott Isaksen and Donald Treffinger combed through the research on practical use of CPS over fifty years, they concluded that CPS made contributions to complex creative tasks and challenges across a variety of situations and contexts. People exposed to CPS used parts of the overall process based on their assessment of how the ideas or stages might help them deal with a particular task or challenge. People also used CPS to clarify their understanding of problems, generate ideas, and create action plans (Isaksen and Treffinger 2004).

creative problem-solving principles

CPS operates on four core principles (Creative Education Foundation 2011):

- **Balance convergent and divergent thinking.** Identify when and how to generate potential solutions (divergent thinking) and when and how to evaluate, choose, and implement those ideas (convergent thinking). This takes time as well as trial and error.

- **Present problems as questions.** When you describe a problem as an open-ended question, you give yourself the opportunity to think about it creatively, with an eye to solving the dilemma. So, instead of saying, "I cannot do this math problem," you might ask, "What things can I do differently to approach this math problem?"

- **Delay judgment of your first idea.** Just keep brainstorming. When you're in the middle of brainstorming, remember the power of yet: you don't have the solution *yet*. Once you have a few ideas, then you can start evaluating them.

- **Say "yes, and" rather than "yes, but."** *Yes, and* encourages people to expand their thoughts. *Yes, but* ends conversation and often negates what came before it.

In 2011 the Creative Education Foundation, a nonprofit organization that uses CPS to empower people to develop new ideas and address problems, presented a modified CPS model. This model has four stages: clarify, ideate, develop, and implement. Together with TOVO's three Cs (cognition, competition, and character), these ideas form a Talent Development Zone for fostering creativity.

TDZ6 To-Do List

To create a Talent Development Zone that develops and inspires creativity in kids, adults need to take these steps with the kids:

- clarify the problem
- brainstorm
- develop solutions
- implement a plan of action
- build cognition
- build competence
- build character

Creative Problem-Solving Thinking
Clarify the Problem

- *Identify the goal or the challenge.* Kids need to identify what their problem actually is in order to look for solutions. In the context of talent development, perhaps a child is falling short in some areas and the goal is to get better at those areas. Be patient so as to identify the correct problem.

- *Gather information.* Take notes on relevant information in order to get a clear understanding of the problem. This could include observations of what is happening as well as feelings about what is going on (yours, the child's, those of other adults involved).

- *Ask questions that will help generate solutions.* Ask the child, "What are you doing to reach your goal? What could you be doing?"

Brainstorm

- Discuss and jot down creative ideas for how to approach the problem.
- Keep brainstorming until you can't think of any more ideas.
- Don't judge the ideas; just collect them. No idea is out of bounds.

Develop Solutions

- Evaluate all the options you and the child came up with through brainstorming.
- Take your time analyzing potential solutions. Do they meet the needs of the child? Can the child implement these changes?

Implement a Plan of Action

- Choose a solution.
- Together with the child, identify what resources and actions will allow them to implement the chosen solution.
- Write down the plan. Make sure it includes clear, achievable steps.

TOVO Thinking
Build Cognition

- Help kids **perceive** and make sense of new information. You can do this by setting up your environment to give kids choices and allowing them to work through those choices on their own—getting some of them right and some wrong. Along the way, they may ask you questions. As they do, empower them and gently guide them to a solution that makes sense in that context.

- Help kids **conceive** of ways to solve problems. Ask questions and use their answers to gently steer them toward discovery of solutions.

- Provide opportunities to **decide and deceive** and **execute** the skill. Avoid being judgmental or overly critical, so kids can build their motivation and confidence. Over time, this will help them develop the courage and the ability to think creatively.

- Give kids a chance to **assess** this process. Accurate assessment is a matter of self-awareness. Kids have varying degrees of self-awareness and may need to develop it. Once kids can honestly and kindly assess their efforts (neither inflating their performance nor beating themselves up), this will free their minds to make the necessary adjustments for next time.

Build Competence

- Provide opportunities for kids to understand that they have progressed in the skill they are trying to improve. Often, skill-building progress is gradual and isn't noticed by the child. As kids learn to read better, play a note more smoothly, or throw a baseball more accurately, make a point of letting them know that they are progressing. Provide some information about where they were and where they are now and how their work got them there.

- Take notes or show kids video of themselves. Sometimes when adults try to help kids understand that they are getting more proficient or competent, the feedback is too ambiguous. Make it concrete, using details from your notes. Perhaps show them a video of their skill before they started practicing and after. Or show them actual growth in their musical skill or comfort in reading via video or audio.

Build Character

- Building character in kids requires a deliberate, everyday approach to implementing your core values. Core values may be things like respect, hard work, honesty, and so on. If you haven't already, you need to name and define your core values, talk about them with your colleagues and the kids, model them, and hold people accountable to them. Doing these things takes them from just words to core values that build character.

TDZ7
BUILD "I CAN" KIDS

Confidence is the feeling or belief that you can rely on yourself, on someone else, or on your circumstances. In kids who have just received the message *you aren't good enough*, self-confidence may take a hit. In fact, at that point many kids are just done. They give up developing that talent because the information hurts, and they don't know how to work through it. Their belief in themselves disintegrates. But it doesn't have to be this way. Here's a true story that illustrates why.

In the 1850s, a little boy in Michigan named Thomas Alva Edison was having a tough time in school. This boy was hard of hearing, which made it difficult to learn at his school. In addition, he was prone to distraction, and to distracting others, in the classroom. He asked too many questions. A teacher called him "addled" and said it wasn't worthwhile keeping him in school any

> The power of a parent, teacher, or coach in helping a child build self-belief can be critical. By guiding kids through tough times, we help them establish that belief.

longer. Edison burst out crying, went home, and told his mother what happened. Edison's mom brought him back to school and "angrily told the teacher that he didn't know what he was talking about" and that her boy had more brains than the teacher himself (O'Connor 1907). She promptly pulled him from school and educated him at home. She found that he was actually quite bright when supported and offered different opportunities to learn. This belief in young Edison from a trusted adult in turn inspired self-belief in his own talent. In an interview decades later, Edison recalled, "She was the most enthusiastic champion a boy ever had, and I determined right then that I would be worthy of her and show her that her confidence was not misplaced" (O'Connor 1907).

This slice of history illustrates the point that self-belief is important in developing one's talent and striving for high-quality performance—and that the power of a parent, teacher, or coach in helping a child build self-belief can be critical. By guiding kids through tough times, we help them establish that belief. We can look at a difficult situation together and let it sting for just long enough to learn from it, without allowing it to completely undermine the kid's confidence. Over time, and through using the suggestions in this chapter, we can teach kids to believe in their innate ability to learn, grow, and improve as they pursue their talents.

Understanding Confidence

Confidence is a catch-all term with many shades of meaning. *Self-confidence* refers to someone's belief in their personal worth and their likelihood of succeeding. A related term, *self-efficacy*, refers to belief about one's ability to perform specific tasks. The concept of self-efficacy comes from social cognitive theory, developed by psychologist Albert Bandura. Bandura defines self-efficacy as "people's beliefs about their capabilities to produce designated levels of performance that exercise influence over events that affect their lives" (Bandura 1994).

Just as many people use a trainer and nutritionist to inform a fitness plan, a confidence development plan for young people can be enhanced by an adult who understands how the elements of a plan work together and how to aid the process by keeping the kid on task, motivated, and excited.

Research on self-efficacy shows that people with higher self-efficacy have higher motivation, put in more effort, have greater resilience, think more productively, and show lower stress and depression. Conversely, people with lower self-efficacy tend to shy away from difficult tasks, are pessimistic about obstacles in their lives, have a lower commitment to their goals, and show greater vulnerability to stress and depression (Bandura 2011).

Bandura's research shows that people's self-efficacy depends on what he calls "sources of self-efficacy." These are the building blocks of self-efficacy—of confidence. Bandura says that if you have, find, or create opportunities to engage in these sources, then you can build more self-efficacy and be more confident.

To illustrate this concept, let's compare it with fitness. If you want to get more fit, what would you do? You might design a plan to (1) eat healthier and more nutritious foods, (2) do a specific amount of strength-training exercises per day or per week, (3) do a certain amount of cardio exercises per day or week, and for good measure (4) toss in some yoga to aid core strength and mental health. These four elements of your plan would be your building blocks of fitness, or your sources of fitness.

Just as many people use a trainer and nutritionist to inform a fitness plan, a confidence development plan for young people can be enhanced by an adult who understands how the elements of a plan work together and how to aid the process by keeping the kid on task, motivated, and excited. As an adult working with kids to develop their talent, you can be a confidence trainer using these sources of self-efficacy:

- mastery or previous successful experiences
- verbal persuasion
- modeling
- emotional and physical readiness

In this chapter we focus on the first two sources: mastery and verbal persuasion. For an in-depth discussion of modeling, see the section of TDZ2 titled "Find Role Models and Show Them to Kids." For more on emotional and physical readiness, see TDZ8.

As you learn about the sources of self-efficacy, think in terms of how you might help a child build physical strength as their personal trainer. One lift, and the person seeking to get fit doesn't suddenly grow exponentially stronger. But lift after lift after lift, these efforts build on one another and increase strength. Like strength training, a methodical process of confidence building, while time consuming, is the most effective approach.

Mastery or Previous Successful Experiences

Mastery is what happens when someone is working at a task or skill and improves on their work or does it correctly. For example, a child works at playing a song on the violin or performing a football pass correctly. The kid finally gets it right. This is a "strength gain moment" or a "mastery experience." When kids do something well and they know it, their confidence increases on the next attempt. They have greater self-belief because of their previous successful experience.

But is a successful experience always a win or a top grade or a perfect sports move or a flawless song? No—a successful experience has a lot to do with how you perceive success. Sometimes kids don't get the result they are aiming for, but they improve. Small improvements are important too, and they also count as successes. Just as small strength gains move a person toward fitness, so do small skill improvements lead to greater confidence.

In TDZ1 we discussed achievement goal theory and how important it is for kids to perceive themselves as successful. The idea is to define success in process terms (getting better, working hard, trying hard, improving relative to their own previous performance) instead of product terms (winning; being better than

> When kids do something well and they know it, they have greater self-belief because of their previous successful experience. Small improvements are important too, and they also count as successes.

others; getting the best grade, score, rank, or time). Achieving wins and surpassing others will happen, and you can use those events as opportunities to bolster confidence, but wins can be few and far between. They may also depend on a variety of factors out of a kid's control. By contrast, process-oriented previous successes are more frequent and more attainable. They build on one another to strengthen confidence over time. They are like incremental daily exercise, which leads to a more fit person.

Verbal Persuasion (and a Bit of Modeling)

Verbal persuasion is communicating with a trusted person about one's capabilities. Let's go back to the fitness analogy. If you are trying to get more fit, but on a particular day you are feeling tired and unmotivated to get your workout done, how do you decide whether to keep going or stop? You might have an internal conversation. In your mind, you weigh the reasons to either keep after it or quit. Or, if you are lucky, you have a trainer who helps you push through. And so it is with verbal persuasion and confidence in kids. Kids engage in self-talk, and others engage in talk with kids. Both approaches can build confidence (or tear it down).

Verbal Persuasion from Adults

Words from adults can influence how confident a child is. Using positive verbal persuasion can lead kids to be more confident, persist at a task, and enjoy it more, which can in turn lead to greater success. Using negative verbal persuasion can lead kids to be less confident and less persistent and enjoy a task less, which can in turn lead to lower success.

The level of the speaker's credibility directly influences the effectiveness of verbal persuasion. When a kid trusts the person giving feedback, the person has more credibility, and as a result also has greater influence. Research suggests that while verbal persuasion may be a weaker source of self-efficacy than mastery experiences, it is still widely used because of its ease and ready availability (Redmond 2016).

If adults can provide some high-quality, positive, well-timed feedback to a child, they can enhance the child's self-efficacy. "Feedback . . . is information about a person's performance of a task used as a basis for improvement" (Lucas 2019). Remember, mastery experiences are the first source of self-efficacy, and feedback can assist with mastery. Recall also that competence is a driving force in motivation; if adults can provide high-quality feedback, then they can foster motivation as well as confidence.

John Hattie is a professor of education at the Melbourne Graduate School of Education at the University of Melbourne in Australia. Much of the research that Dr. Hattie and his colleagues did early in his career focused on the impact of feedback on kids in the classroom. They assert, "Feedback is one of the most powerful influences on learning and achievement" (Hattie and Timperley 2007). They note that when errors are welcomed, feedback is more effective, and that the type of feedback that's effective depends on the level of mastery. At the novice level, people need immediate feedback. At the intermediate level, people need alternative strategies. At the advanced level, people need self-regulated learning (Hattie and Yates 2014).

Valerie Shute, a colleague of Hattie, offers several research-based strategies to enhance student learning (Shute 2008):

- Focus feedback on the task, not the learner.
- Provide specific, clear feedback.
- Provide feedback in manageable chunks.
- Keep feedback as simple as possible, but not too simple.
- Provide objective feedback—written, if possible.
- Provide feedback soon after the learner attempted the skill.

If adults want to enhance a child's confidence through verbal persuasion, they can't provide positive comments all the time. High-quality, timely, honest, constructive, realistic comments from trusted adults enhance confidence. Adults also have a part to play in the development of verbal self-persuasion.

Verbal Self-Persuasion or Self-Talk

All people talk to themselves. (Some do the talking out loud, but all of us talk internally.) Some people take control of that self-talk and use it to help themselves. Some people beat themselves up with their self-talk, which is not helpful at all. Are you aware of what you say to yourself—especially when things aren't going well?

> High-quality, timely, honest, constructive, realistic comments from trusted adults enhance confidence.

Unfortunately, the majority of self-talk is negative, and these negative thoughts create feelings of frustration, anger, hopelessness, and disappointment. But when self-talk is positive, people have lower stress, feel less frustrated, have better coping skills in times of distress, and have better psychological well-being.

When kids hear variations of "You aren't good enough," some will multiply it by telling themselves all kinds of negative self-talk:

- "I am terrible. I am never going to get this done."
- "I am stupid and useless."
- "Why do I even try? I am never going to get it."
- "No matter how hard I work, I'll never succeed."

By contrast, some kids may instead use variations of the following examples of positive self-talk:

- "I didn't get it this time, but I will next time."
- "I wasn't good today, but if I keep working, I can improve."
- "I can do this."
- "I've got this."

Adults play a role in shaping kids' self-talk. And of course, adults can also help change negative self-talk to positive self-talk.

Educational psychologist Paul Burnett conducted a study on children's self-talk and the impact of teachers' statements on it. He collected data on 269 Australian primary school children in grades three to seven. He measured students' perceptions of the frequency of positive and negative statements directed to them by their teacher, as well as their positive and negative self-talk. He found that positive statements made by teachers were directly related to positive self-talk in children, and negative statements made by teachers were predictive of negative self-talk for boys (Burnett 1999).

When adults use positive statements, so do kids—and when adults use negative statements, kids do too.

Practically speaking, when adults say things to kids, it programs kids' self talk. You may recall this quote from TDZ4: "What we speak becomes the house we live in." The research shows that this is true. When adults use positive statements, so do kids—and when adults use negative statements, kids do too.

But once kids have a pattern of negative self-talk, can they change it? I teach athletes to do this all the time. The research on adults in sports is pretty clear: identifying negative self-talk and changing that talk to positive is not only doable but necessary if athletes are to compete at the highest level. But what about in kids?

Kamal Chopra conducted a yearlong series of lessons on self-talk at the University of Lethbridge and learned how to identify specific negative and positive words and affirmations. She found that children needed to learn and understand a three-level process in order to identify negative self-talk and acquire positive self-talk (Chopra 2012):

1. Develop awareness of self-talk, both positive and negative.

2. Develop strategies to change negative self-talk into positive self-talk.

3. Incorporate positive self-talk into daily interactions.

Taken together, the findings of Hattie, Timperley, Yates, Shute, Burnett, and Chopra show us that kids' self-talk is largely programmed by the words they hear, and that kids can indeed change their self-talk.

TDZ7 To-Do List

To create a Talent Development Zone that fosters confidence in kids, adults need to:

- build mastery and previous successful experiences
- use verbal persuasion

Build Mastery and Previous Successful Experiences

- **Help children attribute success to internal, stable factors such as their effort.** Reward and model statements like *I got an A on my test because I am smart and know how to study* and *I scored well because I have been working on my shooting skills.*

- **Give children opportunities to experience mastery.** Make tasks challenging but doable.

- **Catch kids doing well.** When you notice kids doing things right, praise them for it. Talk specifically about *what* was done well and *why.* This makes the success replicable.

Use Verbal Persuasion

- **Be aware of what you are saying to kids both positively and negatively.** Think before you speak, and take time to reflect after you speak.

- **Help kids be aware of negative self-talk.** When you hear kids say things about themselves that are negative, such as *I can't, I will never get this*, or *I always . . .* , chat with them about how they feel when they hear themselves say this.

- **Give kids ideas for positive phrases to say.** Brainstorm some go-to phrases that feel comfortable for children to say. Write these down.

- **Model positive self-talk.** One of the sources of self-efficacy is modeling. Kids learn by watching and listening. Let kids hear you talking positively to yourself. Try to avoid negative phrases like *I can't* and *I never*. Instead, say things like *I know this was hard but I can try it again* and *I can't do it . . . yet*.

TDZ8
HELP KIDS MANAGE PRESSURE

Imagine you are carrying something heavy as you walk from one place to another, navigating obstacles like stairs, doorways, and corners. You feel pressure literally weighing you down as you move. Now imagine somebody comes along to help you carry your load, or simply to encourage you as you go. Do you suppose you might move a little faster or more smoothly, or have a more positive outlook? You probably would. It is always a bit easier to meet a challenge when you have someone in your corner—even if that someone just explains what is happening and tells you that your struggles and mistakes are normal. So it is with kids as they develop their talents.

It is always a bit easier to meet a challenge when you have someone in your corner—even if that someone just explains what is happening and tells you that your struggles and mistakes are normal.

In this chapter, we discuss different kinds of pressure; how we feel pressure; and how we can help kids recognize pressure, manage it, and turn it to their advantage. We build on the ideas and advice about confidence in TDZ7 (Build "I Can" Kids) to build emotional and physical readiness to handle pressure.

Understanding Pressure

First, let's define a few key stress-related terms:

- **"Good" stress is called** *eustress.* It is associated with the term *arousal.*
- **"Bad" stress is called** *distress.* It is often associated with *anxiety.*
- **Stress manifests in two ways—mentally and physically:**
  - Mental manifestation can result in disrupted sleep and in behaviors like self-talk based on one's interpretation of emotions or events or through mental images about what is happening.
  - Physical manifestations are body changes like increased heart rate or breathing and body language.

The relationship between stress and performance can be explained by the inverted-U model (also known as the Yerkes-Dodson law) introduced by psychologists Robert Yerkes and John Dodson. It depicts the relationship between stress (or arousal) and performance (Yerkes and Dodson 1908). See **the diagram below.** This model shows that optimal stress levels in a performance setting are achieved when the performer feels some stress but not too much, and as a result has just the right amount of "electricity" inside to be "in the zone." The optimal stress level is unique to each person. It depends not only on temperament but also on skill level (experience level) at the task. If our skill level is low, we need less stress to perform well. If our skill level is high, we need more stress to perform well.

Stress is "good" (eustress) until it isn't. When stress turns "bad," it becomes distress. That turning point varies from person to person. The body feels the stress rising and interprets it mentally and physically. As stress rises, at first we may think, "I've got this. No big deal." And then something happens, and suddenly our thinking changes: "Get me out of here!"

Here's a quick example to illustrate the crossover from eustress to distress. A girl is playing in a championship volleyball match. She enters the game feeling like she is a decent athlete and that her team is playing a pretty good opponent. (Her perceived stress level in this case relates both to her perception of her own ability level as well as her perception of her opponents' abilities.) The game starts, and the girl feels like she is getting into it. She is starting to do some good things—passing well, moving her feet well, and communicating effectively. She is physiologically engaged too; her heart rate and breathing both quicken. Then she makes a mistake, missing an easy pass to her teammate that causes her team to lose the point. Her stress level starts to rise. It prompts her to focus harder on the match. She is in the zone of optimal stress and best performance.

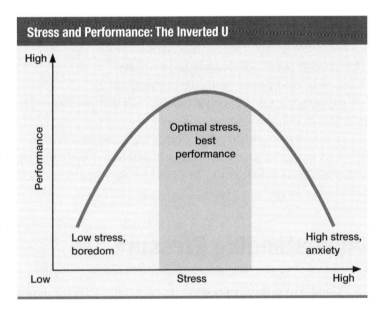

But then she makes another passing error, and this one leads to her team losing the set. The girl thinks, "I can't believe I did that! I always do that. This is awful. I am a terrible player." Then she makes another mistake, and another, and another. She is distressed.

For each individual working on a specific task or skill set, there is an optimal amount of stress required to produce optimal performance. In fact, growth and learning cannot happen without stress. For example, when a weightlifter wants to get stronger, they have to lift weights. But lifting the same weight a few times a day for eight weeks won't build strength because it isn't stressing the muscles. To get stronger, the weightlifter must lift heavier weights, do more repetitions, use different exercises, and so on in a methodical and safe way. They must stress their muscles. Likewise, for students, musicians, athletes, and all other performers to develop their talents, they must experience some stress.

When children are comfortable and confident in a performance domain, then they can handle more stress. When children are new to a skill and have low confidence, then they need minimal amounts of stress to perform well. They gradually build the skill under gradually increasing pressure.

Managing pressure is a learned skill; it's neither innate nor fixed. In other words, people can get better at managing stress. Some folks may start out with the ability to handle a bit more pressure than others can, but *everyone* can learn coping skills to learn to better manage stress. In the volleyball example, a coach could help the girl see that she is saying negative things to herself and that those words are causing stress, and then teach her some ways to manage her self-talk. This in turn would help her manage that stress, which would have a positive impact on her performance.

For each individual working on a specific task or skill set, there is an optimal amount of stress required to produce optimal performance. In fact, growth and learning cannot happen without stress.

For kids to develop their talents, they must feel a healthy amount of discomfort in the effort. If they don't leave their comfort zone, then they aren't learning anything new. It's uncomfortable not to make a team, to fail a test, or not to receive a callback after an audition. The trick is to embrace that discomfort and keep trying. There will be times when kids are putting in loads of deep, deliberate practice and still failing. At these times, kids may cross over from eustress to distress if they don't have adequate coping skills. If adults can help kids be aware of when and how they are becoming mentally or physically distressed and give them some coping skills, then kids will have a better chance of staying on the path to develop their talents.

TDZ8 **To-Do List**

To create a Talent Development Zone that helps kids manage pressure, adults need to:

- build kids' self-awareness about the pressure they are feeling
- help kids use self-talk to manage emotions
- teach kids to manage the body to manage the mind

Build Kids' Self-Awareness About the Pressure They Are Feeling

Several decades ago, psychologists Shelley Duval and Robert Wicklund developed a theory of objective self-awareness. This theory says that "when we focus our attention on ourselves, we evaluate and compare our current behavior to our internal standards and values. We become self-conscious as objective evaluators of ourselves" (Duval and Wicklund 1972).

Ken Ravizza, a noted performance psychology expert, took this idea of self-awareness a step further as he applied it to athletes. In his book *Heads-Up Baseball: Playing the Game One Pitch at a Time*, he describes self-awareness as a person's ability to be aware of their emotions in order to perform at their best. He proposes that self-awareness is the key to cognitive control.

Ravizza uses the idea of a traffic light to give people a visual representation of their stress level and their stress management. A green light means they are in the eustress zone. A red light means they are feeling distressed. A yellow light means they are in the right zone to use coping skills and reduce their stress level.

As adults helping kids develop their talents, we want kids to be aware of their emotions. But often, when we ask children how they feel, they don't know—or can't explain it. So, simply asking kids how they feel when the situation has become or is getting chaotic usually isn't effective. The key is to establish a baseline of emotional awareness in order to manage stress later. Here are a few ideas for how to raise kids' awareness of their feelings:

- **Ask kids how they feel** at different times—when they're at their best, when they are frustrated, and when they perform poorly.

- **Have kids write down how they felt** in a moment of pressure.

- **Encourage kids to watch others** perform on stage, on TV, in sports, and so on and ask them how they think that person feels and if they are managing pressure.

Help Kids Use Self-Talk to Manage Emotions

We've discussed the concept of self-talk in the context of practice (TDZ3), optimism (TDZ4), and confidence (TDZ7). In the context of stress, kids need to combine awareness and self-talk to manage pressure. Here's how:

- **Help kids be aware that they are feeling pressure.** Help them identify whether they are at a green, red, or yellow light in the moment.

- **Help kids be aware of what they are saying and when they are saying it.** Ask them questions after their performance or give them a heads-up to pay attention to their self-talk. Have them take notes afterward. Look at these notes later and assess whether they were helpful or hurtful to their performance.

- **Help kids change their self-talk.** Create some go-to phrases for kids to use when they are at a red light. Write down these phrases and post them where they'll be noticed. Help kids use these phrases whenever they feel pressure. When you see kids getting frustrated, use these words yourself. And after the fact, review with them what happened.

Teach Kids to Manage the Body to Manage the Mind

Body language can have a profound effect on how the body interprets stress. That is, some body movements foster eustress, while others encourage distress. We can teach kids to use the former instead of the latter to manage their stress level.

Amy Cuddy is a Harvard Business School professor, social psychologist, and author of the book *Presence: Bringing Your Boldest Self to Your Biggest Challenges*. In the book, she describes her research on body language—specifically, the impact of people's nonverbal expressions on stress and confidence.

Cuddy studied levels of testosterone (a hormone that promotes dominance or confidence) and cortisol (a stress hormone) in people as they held either a power pose (standing straight with hands in the air in the shape of a V or hands to sides) or a non–power pose (arms folded, curled up, arm on neck). Subjects were asked to hold the pose for two minutes prior to going into a job interview. In the interview, subjects answered a series of questions. They gave saliva samples after the interview to test for testosterone and cortisol levels.

Cuddy found that when people stood in power positions, they raised their own testosterone levels and decreased their cortisol levels. Conversely, those standing in non–power positions had higher cortisol and lower testosterone levels. In other words, she essentially found that if people manage their body language prior to going into a stressful situation, they can change the stress levels in their body. They can change the body to change the mind.

This is useful information for adults teaching kids to manage stress. You can help them by:

- raising their awareness of their body language by asking them about it and showing them with video recordings

- modeling helpful body language when you are under stress

- challenging them to notice others showing helpful body language

- encouraging them to display helpful body language before they engage in an exam, a practice, or any performance endeavor

TDZ9
DEVELOP GRIT (AND KNOW WHEN TO CHANGE COURSE)

Think of something you love to do that took you a long time to get good at. Perhaps it's your job. Maybe it's a sport or playing a musical instrument or chess. Chances are, on your way to being good at this endeavor, you encountered all the mental obstacles we have discussed so far, including

> Success takes a steadfast determination to not give up.

feeling pessimistic, unmotivated, unconfident, stressed out, uncreative, and stymied by a perceived glass ceiling. On this journey you may even have thought about quitting. But you didn't. You persisted, persevered, and kept on keeping on.

Success takes a steadfast determination to not give up. Think about the successful people mentioned throughout this book, such as Dav Pilkey, Maya Angelou, Michael Jordan, Thomas Edison, and Harry Kane, who persisted over time in the face of failure. They all demonstrated long-term perseverance, or grit. Grit is "firmness of mind or spirit; unyielding courage in the face of hardship or danger" (merriam-webster.com). Neurobiologist Angela Duckworth defines grit as "passion and perseverance for long-term goals" (Duckworth, n.d).

Understanding Grit

Duckworth is author of the book *Grit: The Power of Passion and Perseverance*. Duckworth's work, which she explains in this book, has had a profound impact across academic disciplines and in US culture. It has sparked important debates about learning, development, achievement, resilience, talent, conscientiousness, and related concepts in scientific and education circles.

In her book, she explores why some folks are successful at endeavors in which many others fail or drop out. One example she describes is that of twelve hundred US Military Academy West Point cadets in their quest to complete a seven-week summer training program prior to their freshman year. It's a grueling program called Beast Barracks: cadets labor in the classroom and outdoors for seventeen hours a day with no breaks except meals. Duckworth wanted to know why some made it through and some dropped out. Even though the school has a rigorous admissions screening process that includes weighted SAT or ACT scores, personality tests, fitness tests, and high school rank, these assessment tools could not reliably predict who would make it through Beast and who would quit.

Duckworth designed and administered a test for cadets that measured their passion and their willingness to persevere in the pursuit of long-term goals. She called it the Grit Scale. She found that the Grit Scale was the only accurate predictor of cadet success or failure. (You can view long and short versions of Duckworth's Grit Scale at her website, angeladuckworth.com.) Later, she found the same predictor—a combination of passion and perseverance, or grit—in spelling bee champions, elite athletes, Green Berets, high school graduates, and higher-level academics.

> Talent needs to be combined with effort in order for talent to transform into skill. Skill, in turn, needs to be combined with more effort in order to transform into achievement.

In a comprehensive literature review, researchers at the University of Bolton in the United Kingdom found that grit was linked with academic achievement. Grit correlated with perseverance at challenging tasks, academic performance and achievement, goal orientation, motivation in academics, and amount of time studying. Grit was also positively linked with self-esteem and self-efficacy (confidence), growth mindset, managing stress, and feelings of satisfaction (Kannangara et al. 2018).

But how does grit work? Duckworth's research convinced her that talent alone isn't enough—effort is the key to developing talent:

talent × effort = skill

skill × effort = achievement

As you can see from this formula, effort counts twice in the journey toward achievement. Talent needs to be combined with effort in order to transform into skill. Skill, in turn, needs to be combined with more effort in order to transform into achievement.

In this book, we've discussed the importance of effort at length. Effort plays a key role in embracing failure as an opportunity (TDZ1), fostering in kids a love for their endeavors (TDZ5), building "I can" kids (TDZ7), and managing pressure (TDZ8). What's new here is a discussion of the kind of effort that leads to *long-term* passion and perseverance. Duckworth suggests that there are two distinct ways to develop grit: from the inside out and from the outside in. This chapter focuses on developing grit from the inside out. (We discuss doing so from the outside in—through a culture of development—in the next chapter.)

Developing Grit from the Inside Out

Duckworth proposes that four components are critical to building grit from the inside out: interest, practice, purpose, and hope.

- **Interest:** If there is no interest in an endeavor, there is no passion to pursue it, and therefore no grit. Conversely, an intrinsic passion keeps a person going when adversity hits. As we discussed in TDZ5 on motivation, it is critical that kids learn to love what they do. Kids who are interested in what they are doing are likely to keep at it—to persevere.

- **Practice:** Duckworth points out that practice is vital to sustaining interest over time and persevering in the face of adversity, setbacks, and failures. (For more on deep, deliberate practice, see TDZ3.)

- **Purpose:** Purpose is feeling that your work matters, both to you and to the world. To illustrate why purpose is important, let's recount the parable of the bricklayers: Three bricklayers are working away on the same structure. A passerby asks each bricklayer, "What are you doing?" The first says, "I am laying bricks." The second says, "I am building a church." The third says, "I am building the house of god." Duckworth explains, "The first bricklayer has a job. The second has a career. The third has a calling" (Duckworth 2016, 149). For kids developing their talents, the journey will have many twists and turns and ups and downs. But if they believe their work is important to themselves and their world, they will persevere in the face of adversity.

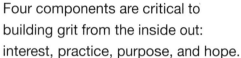

Four components are critical to building grit from the inside out: interest, practice, purpose, and hope.

- **Hope:** Hope is the belief that you can improve and reach your long-term goals. Hope helps sustain passion through the power of optimism. (For more on optimism, see TDZ4.) Optimism encourages you to believe that you can—and that it's worth the effort to—overcome setbacks and persevere. A growth mindset is an important aspect of hope. If you have a growth mindset and you hit a roadblock, you believe that you can grow and change and overcome that obstacle. You don't attribute the problem to permanent personal traits. (For more on growth mindset, see TDZ1.)

We've already discussed each of these four concepts in other chapters of this book. So why does grit get its own chapter? If you reread each of the preceding bullet points, you will see a common thread: perseverance.

Perseverance

Perseverance is persistence in doing something despite difficulty or delay in achieving success. Pursuing talent, a lifelong personal journey often peppered with the word *no* and full of obstacles, takes perseverance. But what exactly is perseverance, and how can it be built?

Dig deep inside for a memory about yourself in which you persevered over time to achieve something difficult. Perhaps it was a shorter period of time, such as in learning a dance move, memorizing your lines for a play, trying to win a game of chess, or studying to get an A on an exam.

Or maybe it was a longer period of time, such as in completing a degree program, winning a chess championship, or performing an entire dance routine. Each small moment of perseverance can lead to larger perseverance over a longer period of time.

If someone were to describe these moments of perseverance, what would they say about you? I propose that they mean you were being competitive. But how does perseverance equate to competition?

Competition

If you are to truly persevere, then you in fact must compete—possibly against others, but mostly against yourself. Often the biggest obstacle to overcome in a long-term pursuit isn't the doubt of others, it is your own doubt. In the context of grit, to compete means to put forth all your effort toward your *interest*, through deep, deliberate *practice*, because you have *purpose*—you believe this work matters—and you're *hopeful* that you will achieve a successful outcome if you *persevere* in the face of adversity. Competing is necessary to develop your talent. When you compete for what you want, it means you care about what you are pursuing. You might feel nervous, or frustrated when things don't go right, but you push through your doubts and keep going.

Why Competition? How Is It Different from Effort?

Effort means simply trying, while *competition* means trying to beat someone or something— possibly yourself. To compete is to strive to gain or win something by defeating or establishing superiority over others who are trying to do the same, or by besting your own achievements. If I tell a kid "Give effort," I'm saying "Give more or try more." If I say "Have grit," it probably won't mean much to a kid because it's too broad and abstract a concept. But if I say "Compete," a kid often has a visceral reaction. The word *compete* adds a concrete punch to the idea of giving effort. When we compete, we are trying to beat something.

Children compete on a daily basis. How many times have you seen a child competing in a dribbling game during practice or in a one-on-one game, or striving for a higher score than a classmate, or working toward the honor of first chair in the band? During these times children are competing; they are being persistent at the task in order to be *successful*. But competing needn't always be against someone else. In fact, I am advocating that we adults create environments that help kids compete against themselves instead of others.

When kids compete against themselves, they strive to beat their own past performance. Adults can encourage self-referenced improvement instead of other-referenced improvement. We can emphasize working hard over being the best. (See TDZ1 for more about the benefits of this approach.)

We as adults can help foster and reward healthy self-competitiveness in children as they develop their talents by how we interact with them in moments of adversity. This doesn't mean winding kids up to be perfectionists or to get angry if they don't get the results they want. That's poor emotion management in the face of adversity. The goal isn't to criticize kids if they aren't getting the desired results. Rather, the goal is to nurture and reward them at key times to encourage grit. To find out how, see the TDZ9 To-Do List at the end of this chapter.

Changing Course

Is it possible to have too much grit? Asked another way: is there a point in the quest to develop a talent when it makes more sense to stop being gritty? Is it okay to quit and change direction?

Let's say you've been working hard for a long time at a sport, a business venture, or a college major. You fail over and over and try again over and over. Eventually you decide to quit, pivot, and start doing something else. And to your delight, you discover that giving up your original pursuit was the best thing to happen to you. For example, after you quit golf, maybe you start to play tennis and are very successful. Or you get out of the dry-cleaning business and start a lawn-care business and crush it. Perhaps you change your major from sociology to psychology—and it just clicks. This sort of thing happens more often than you might think.

Noted career development author Seth Godin wrote a book called *The Dip: A Little Book That Teaches You When to Quit (and When to Stick)*. In it he discusses how changing domains—or quitting—may in fact be a good thing in the pursuit of greatness. He argues that folks who achieve great success in sports, work, and so on quit quickly once they figure out that their trajectory is not the best fit for them. He points out that when people hit a rough patch, many don't take the time to figure out whether it's a temporary setback (a dip) that they should push through or a dead end (a cul-de-sac) that isn't worth the effort. "Quitting at the right time is difficult," he says. "Most of us don't have the guts to quit" (Godin 2007, 43). Godin doesn't suggest that folks shouldn't try hard or give their all or persevere in the face of failure. Rather, he suggests that people should be flexible enough to quit and change course when they feel something isn't the right fit or isn't going to serve their long-term goals or view of themselves.

> People should be flexible enough to quit and change course when they feel something isn't the right fit or isn't going to serve their long-term goals or view of themselves.

In his book *Range*, David Epstein describes this idea as match quality. *Match quality* is a term used by economists that refers to how well someone's job fits who they are as a person. Epstein cites example after example of people being happier and showing more growth when they switch jobs or even industries—so long as they gained some lived experience in the job or industry or area that they were leaving.

Remember experience-producing drive (EPD) theory? It says human beings are active agents designed to survive in their environment, and as such, they have evolved traits to help facilitate that survival. Over time folks pursue, practice, and acquire skills that fit with their personal drive. But the expression of this drive depends on being exposed to the right environment at the right time, and absence of this timely exposure can impact the development of the individual. In other words, people need to have some lived experience to make an informed decision to be gritty or not.

When does a child have enough lived experience to drop out of one thing and into something else as they develop their talent? There's no single answer to this question, but I can tell you that I see many parents and kids struggle with *should I stay or should I go?* when children are between eleven and fourteen years old. At this age, sports, the arts, and education often start demanding more work and more time in order to keep developing, to reach the next level, and to stay there. When athletes ask me for advice on this topic, I ask them to consider three important questions. (See the TDZ9 To-Do List at the end of this chapter.)

No one can know for sure when the right time is to grit and grind or to stop all together. But providing lived experiences in a healthy, supportive environment can help ensure that decisions are made thoughtfully, not emotionally.

Winston Churchill, prime minister of the United Kingdom during World War II, spoke to the students of Harrow School in October 1941—two years into the war. During this speech he offered advice about quitting that has become famous and is often quoted. But usually people don't include the end of the sentence (in italics here): "Never give in, never give in, never, never, never, never—in nothing, great or small, large or petty—*never give in except to convictions of honor and good sense*" (Churchill 1941). Help kids make decisions based on good sense, and this will surely assist them in their quest for talent.

TDZ9 **To-Do List**

To create a Talent Development Zone that helps kids develop grit from the inside, adults need to:

- nurture and reward kids at key times when they face adversity
- be purposeful
- ask three important questions about changing course

Nurture and Reward Kids at Key Times When They Face Adversity

- **Encourage kids to approach, not avoid.** When children face hard times in talent development, nudge them to keep trying as opposed to avoiding.
- **Challenge kids to compete against themselves.** Have them recall their previous attempt and figure out what they could have done better. Some children will focus on the result instead, or on how terrible they are, or some other extreme. To some degree

this may be part of their personality, but your focus on providing multiple chances to improve their performance (without comparison to others) can help change this attitude slowly but surely.

- **If kids ask for feedback, be honest but tactful.** When children mess up, they don't need to be crushed. Be honest with them but also kind. Express your honest critique in process-oriented terms rather than outcome-oriented terms.

- **When kids compete against others, remind them of their individual goals.** Some kids perform best when they compete against other people in arts, academics, or sports. This isn't inherently bad, but it does need to be managed. These kids thrive on a me-versus-you mentality, and they're over the moon when they win. But when they lose, they may not have the coping skills to manage their emotions. Some kids are very hard on themselves. Remind these kids that the goal is to reach for personal improvement. After a failure, focus on the process, not the product, to encourage persistence. This takes many repetitions for some kids!

Be Purposeful

- **Don't confuse activity with accomplishment.** Sometimes a child just wants to play baseball or read or draw for fun. This enjoyment is good; in fact, it's key for long-term engagement. But if a kid is practicing, then they should be trying to get something out of that practice time. Whether it is improving comprehension or honing a particular skill, goal-oriented behavior is important to improve and to build grit.

- **Encourage kids to challenge themselves.** Part of building grit is to persist in the face of failure. For failures to happen, kids need to challenge themselves purposefully and willingly with harder tasks—and learn to enjoy that challenge. Encourage kids to be purposeful in their approach, and when it is hard, help kids work through uncomfortable feelings. This will allow them to understand that challenge, failure, and discomfort are all normal. They are events that happen on the way to getting good at something. Remind kids that they can come out on the other side of such experiences better than when they went in.

Ask Three Important Questions About Changing Course

- **"Do you love what you're doing?"** In TDZ5, we discussed the importance of kids needing to love what they do. As they toil away at their pursuits, continue to satisfy their innate needs for competence, autonomy, and relatedness. When these three innate needs are met, intrinsic motivation increases and people are more likely to engage in the activity because they want to (rather than because they have to).

- **"If you drop out of this pursuit, what will you drop into?"** As kids pursue their talents, sometimes they get tired and distracted. And sometimes they quit. When kids are determined to quit, encourage them to get into something else. An environment that offers a variety of experiences gives kids not only a healthy approach to skill building but also the knowledge they need to pursue what's next when they're ready to move on.

- **"Are you willing to be a realist *and* an optimist?"** As you may recall from TDZ4, realistic optimism is a clear-eyed, positive attitude. A kid who's a realist and an optimist understands that no amount of positivity will help if they are doing something ineffective. A realistic optimist doesn't give up and doesn't keep doing the same old thing— they adjust their efforts to achieve a new result.

TDZ10
CREATE A CULTURE OF DEVELOPMENT

Culture is critically important to helping kids see and go after their talents. But the word *culture* has many meanings, so let's narrow our focus a bit. If we look at the history of the term, we can see it derives from the idea of cultivating land. This history offers a useful perspective for understanding culture in the context of developing talent. You can view your role of developing children's talents as akin to planting, nurturing, and cultivating crops.

This chapter examines the meaning of *culture* as it pertains to schools, teams, family units, and other groups in society that help people develop their talents. As we discuss a variety of examples and research findings, a working definition of *culture* emerges. The end of the chapter offers practical advice that adults can use to establish a culture of development.

To understand *culture* as part of talent development, there are four parts to examine:

- shared norms and values—how we do things . . .

- expressed with language, heuristics, and the power of stories . . .

- developed through play so learning feels organic . . .

- with safety, vulnerability, and purpose.

Understanding Culture
Shared Norms and Values—How We Do Things

Today's use of the word *culture* is understood to be what a group of people share in values and norms. When your group has an agreed upon way of doing things, that's the group's culture. Culture can grow grit from the outside in—Angela Duckworth devotes an entire chapter of her book *Grit* to culture. To help us connect to creating a culture of development, she says, "A distinct culture exists anytime a group of people are in consensus about how we do things around here and why. As for how the rest of the world operates, the sharper the contrast, the stronger the bonds among those in what psychologists call the 'in-group'" (Duckworth 2016, 244–245).

She recounts a story about Pete Carroll, head coach of the Seattle Seahawks football team, and how he selects and develops players. She also describes the community members associated

> "
>
> The members of organizations with strong cultures are so involved in and intertwined with the group culture that it shapes not only how they do things, but also how they see themselves.

with a school model called KIPP (Knowledge Is Power Program). Both have built strong cultures—so deeply imbedded in the identities of their members that folks don't say they are Seahawks players or KIPP students but rather Seahawks and KIPPsters. The members of these organizations are so involved in and intertwined with the group culture that it shapes not only how they do things, but also how they see themselves.

We can see from these examples how culture shapes our being. And now we have the first piece of our working definition: Culture is **shared norms and values—how we do things.**

Expressed with Language, Heuristics, and the Power of Stories

The All Blacks are New Zealand's national men's rugby team. They compete against other national rugby teams around the globe. They won the 1987, 2011, and 2015 Rugby World Cups. They boast a winning record of 77 percent (New Zealand Rugby, n.d.) and are widely considered to be the winningest team of any sport anywhere in the world (Thomas, n.d.). New Zealand has a population of only 4.5 million people; its human and financial resources are dwarfed by those of other countries. How do the All Blacks do it? They have built a strong culture.

James Kerr, an expert on performance psychology and organizational science (in business and sports), gained unparalleled access to study the All Blacks while writing his book *Legacy: What the All Blacks Can Teach Us About the Business of Life.* What he learned is remarkable, from a culture perspective. Kerr used his observations to develop fifteen lessons in leadership. One of these lessons is about the importance of language in building culture.

Kerr explains that in the 1990s, the All Blacks were disintegrating. That is, the team's longtime standards, expectations, and wins were sinking. When two veteran players, John Kirwan and Sean Fitzpatrick, noticed the problem, they decided to write a book of principles for the team. Fitzpatrick described it as "a system of meanings that everyone understood—a language and vocabulary and a set of beliefs that bound the group together" (Kerr 2013). This book would come to be known as The Black Book and was for All Blacks' eyes only. Its collected wisdom included statements like "No one is bigger than the team," "It's an honor, not a job," and "It's not enough to be good. It's about being great" (Kerr 2013).

The language and vocabulary of beliefs can be used in storytelling, which is a key way to foster culture. Kerr notes that elite groups and organizations tend to have a great story. This story and all its details tell the people within that group, "This is what we stand for, and this is why we stand for it." But of course, key to how a group understands its story is how the story is told. Specific language—including terminology, maxims, and detailed metaphors—provide a connection to the story and help the group connect the story to its core values and everyday goings-on.

In essence, language defines who we are and how we act. Language turns into stories, and these stories tell the reality of what we want and who we are. They make our meaning. Kerr goes on to say that heuristics are a critical piece of culture. He describes heuristics as easily understood and memorizable code-phrases that "go straight to the heart of the belief system, becoming shorthand for the standards and behavior that is expected" (Kerr 2013). This what the Black Book achieved—and it was part of turning the team's fortunes around.

Adam Grant is a psychologist, management expert, and business professor at the Wharton School of the University of Pennsylvania. He agrees about the power of storytelling in building culture. Grant gets invited to visit and advise companies all the time. He reports that they all say, "Our culture is unique!" So he asks how the culture is unique. The answers are always the same: "People really believe in our values and they think that we're a cause, so we're so passionate about the mission!" (Johnson 2018). Grant points out that values and mission are not culture. If a group

> Elite groups and organizations tend to have a great story. This story and all its details tell the people within that group, "This is what we stand for, and this is why we stand for it."

truly has a strong culture, its members should be able to "tell you a story about something that happens in the organization that would not happen anywhere else" (Montag 2017).

So it is with the culture that surrounds a child in pursuit of talent. Kids need strong values, vocabulary, and mottos that are defined and then told through stories—stories that can be discussed in pictures or words; stories that have happened or have yet to happen. And now we have the second piece of our working definition: Culture is shared norms and values—how we do things . . . **expressed with language, heuristics, and the power of stories.**

Developed Through Play So Learning Feels Organic

If something is organic, it is an integral part of the whole. This definition might conjure up the idea that something organic just happens. But nothing just happens, does it? Well, it depends on who you ask.

To a child growing up within a culture, it might indeed seem to be simply "how we do things." Someone who is new to that culture, however, might think "This is how we do things because they *told* me it's how we do things." They don't feel the culture organically in their being, so it isn't an integral part of life to them; rather, it's just a model to follow or a way to get along.

Walk into any academic's house and you will likely find books lying around. In a musician's house, you'll find instruments and musical scores; in a chef's house, a kitchen with lots of equipment; and so on. Kids in these houses see their parents using these items and have access to them. Often they simply pick them up and play with them—organically. If their parents *let them play*, there's a good chance they will enjoy it. Enjoying something is the first step on the way to learning more about it, getting better at it, and developing a passion for it.

Piaget on Child Development

Jean Piaget was a Swiss psychologist known for his work on child development. Piaget theorized that children progress through a series of four cognitive stages, during which their thought processes become increasingly similar to those of adults. In order to move through these stages, children need to play and learn and play and learn repeatedly. Piaget argued that children need to have the opportunity to practice and combine acquired skills to incorporate these skills into their new reality and their new skill set.

Piaget called this process of building skills assimilation and accommodation. When children assimilate, they learn something new and fit it into what they already know. Kids do this through trial and error and play. Once kids have assimilated knowledge, they accommodate it. Accommodation is reshaping the organization of knowledge to make a new reality. For example: Let's say a child learns that *cat* is the word for a furry pet that lives at Grandma's house. The kid starts to call all furry, four-legged animals "cats." This is assimilation of knowledge. The kid calls the furry, four-legged, barking animal in the yard next door a "cat." Dad says, "That's a dog." The kid realizes that cats and dogs are both furry pets, but cats meow while dogs bark. This is accommodation of knowledge.

Why is play so important? Play is activity engaged in for enjoyment and recreation. It is doing something unstructured because you want to, not because you have to. Play is something kids do spontaneously when they have the opportunity. Kids will play at anything they're allowed access to, including sports, intellectual pursuits, and the arts. Play is one of the important ways kids learn and develop.

Lev Vygotsky was a Soviet psychologist who came up with the cultural-historical theory of child development. This theory says that children develop as a result of their interactions with the society and culture around them—including parents, siblings, teachers, classmates, and playmates. Vygotsky's theory says that play helps kids develop their ability to think *and* develop their social and emotional skills, and that these domains are interrelated. Play is a tool that children use to learn about and make sense of new things and concepts.

Vygotsky coined the term *zone of proximal development (ZPD),* which lies between a child's actual level of development (what they can do independently) and their potential development (what they can do with help). He believed that play is "the leading source of development in pre-school years. . . . Play is the source of development and creates the zone of proximal development" (Bodrova and Leong 2015). In the ZPD, a child plays with objects or with others and stretches their development in areas such as self-control, cooperation, memory, and skill. For example, two children are playing with a toy truck. Through trial and error, they figure out that this truck can roll twice as far when they pull it back and then push it. Next they find out that the truck goes even farther when it goes down a ramp or a hill. Then they realize that the truck can carry other toys . . . and so on. The children are completely in charge of this play episode and the resulting development. Vygotsky believed that having a safe place to try out new skills is important in cognitive and emotional development. Adults can provide this safe place, as well as the physical ingredients of play (such as the truck, ramp, and other toys in the example above).

A culture of play for kids of all ages provides a safe place to explore, try, make mistakes, learn, and work on things. Access to a wide variety of materials—books, trucks, balls, musical instruments, cooking gear, or anything else—offers kids a jumping-off point for learning. A child thinks, "Why not? These things are here, I like playing with them, and everyone else seems to like it and let me do it. It must be what we do here."

And now we have the third piece of our working definition: Culture is shared norms and values—how we do things . . . expressed with language, heuristics, and the power of stories . . . **developed through play so learning feels organic.**

A culture of play for kids of all ages provides a safe place to explore, try, make mistakes, learn, and work on things. Access to a wide variety of materials—books, trucks, balls, musical instruments, cooking gear, or anything else—offers kids a jumping-off point for learning.

With Safety, Vulnerability, and Purpose

Vygotsky noted that play is productive when young children feel safe. Daniel Coyle expands on this in his book *The Culture Code: The Secrets of Highly Successful Groups,* where he proposes that successful groups of adults have strong cultures when members build safety, share vulnerability, and establish purpose.

Safety

Humans are social creatures who seek safety. When we feel secure, we can relax and use our energy to get things done instead of to keep ourselves safe. According to behavioral scientist Amy Edmondson, psychological safety is "a shared belief held by members of a team that the team is safe for interpersonal risk taking" (Edmondson 1999).

Coyle points out that a psychologically safe environment is not one in which people never receive tough, truthful, critical feedback. Rather, it's an environment where people do not feel threatened by such feedback. They believe that regardless of the feedback they get, they will remain valued members of the group. In a psychologically safe group, members receive feedback that includes this message: "I'm giving you these comments because I have very high expectations and I know that you can reach them" (Coyle 2018a, 56). This message offers the listener three key safety cues:

- The feedback giver values the receiver.

- The receiver feels positive attention and energy.

- The receiver feels securely part of that group going forward.

Google spent several years conducting research on team effectiveness and found that "Of the five key dynamics of effective teams that the researchers identified, psychological safety was by far the most important" (Google, n.d.).

Kids need the same psychological safety that high-performing adults do. When kids feel safe, they are more likely to strive, take risks, and be vulnerable to feedback and failure in the process. To build safety, adults can do the following:

- Listen.
- Be fallible as a leader.
- Say thank you a lot.
- Make sure everyone has a voice.
- Embrace fun.

Vulnerability

Only after folks feel safe can they be vulnerable. When we are vulnerable, we let our personal guard down, set aside our insecurities, stop trying to cover up our inadequacies, trust each other, and give way to the values and norms of the group in order to get the work of the group done. Coyle explains that "exchanges of vulnerability, which we naturally tend to avoid, are the pathway through which trusting cooperation is built" (Coyle 2018a, 112).

A vulnerability loop is a mutual exchange of openness to risk that builds cooperation and trust. In other words: being vulnerable signals that others can also be vulnerable. Here are some ways adults can create vulnerability in groups when they are working with kids:

- Make sure the leader is vulnerable too.
- Deliver negative or critical information constructively in person, not in writing.
- When you speak, follow it up with action that backs up your words.
- In conversation, try not to just add value without fully listening. First, listen intently to hear the message, then think, then respond.

Purpose

In this book, we have talked about purpose in the context of practice, motivation, and grit. Purpose is also an important aspect of culture.

Coyle describes purpose as a set of extremely clear goals. To build a strong culture, a group needs a shared purpose that is simple and engaging. "Strong cultures work to unearth and expose the core narratives of their group, then drastically overcommunicate those narratives, using every possible mode (story, artifacts around the space, video, slogans, you name it). All that signaling works like emotional GPS to constantly orient the group, and to help them navigate problems together" (Coyle, n.d.).

Let's say you're a music teacher, and you want to create a strong culture and a shared purpose by hammering home your core narratives in a high school jazz vocal ensemble. The first thing you could do is ask the kids to tell a story that happened in the group. They may or may not be able to do this. If they cannot, perhaps you could help and tell a story that happened to the group that you feel encapsulates their spirit. The story could be about their curiosity, their energy, their playfulness, their amazing singing ability, their hard work, or all those things.

Once you've got a story, challenge the kids to identify some words that describe the feelings or qualities shared or felt in the story—*curious, energetic, joyful, enthusiastic, playful, talented, hardworking*, or the like. Hopefully you can come up with three to five words that describe the story and the group. If the kids are having trouble coming up with a story or words from a story, ask them to come up with a few words they'd like to be known for by the end of the year. Either way, these words should encapsulate who they are and who they are striving to be every day as a group. This process starts to establish shared purpose.

One more step allows these words to be easily remembered and as a result, easier to use. Try to come up with one or two short phrases that can serve as a mantra for each word. For example, the mantra for *energetic* could be *positive energy creates harmony*. The idea is to create go-to phrases that remind the group: this is who we are, and this is what we do. You or the kids can say this phrase when you want to amplify and acknowledge harmonious, energetic vibes that are happening or when the group is feeling flat and needs an energy boost.

> To build a strong culture, a group needs a shared purpose that is simple and engaging.

When we provide a safe place for kids to feel vulnerable so they can pursue their purpose, we are in essence providing them a place to be themselves. We as adults can show empathy and vulnerability by letting them know that we are in in this together.

Now we have the fourth and final piece of our working definition: Culture is shared norms and values—how we do things . . . expressed with language, heuristics, and the power of stories . . . developed through play so learning feels organic . . . **with safety, vulnerability, and purpose.**

TDZ10 **To-Do List**

To build a culture of development, adults need to:

- choose vocabulary that defines how the child wants to pursue their talent
- create stories
- let kids play
- build safety
- allow and show vulnerability
- clarify purpose

Choose Vocabulary That Defines How the Child Wants to Pursue Their Talent

- Use words that resonate with them.
- Form some mantras and mottos, such as *be your best, mistakes happen—it's about effort, make failure your fuel*, or *enjoy the journey*.
- Use these words often and post them where you can see them, such as on the fridge, in the locker room, on the bulletin board, or in the car.

Create Stories

- As children pursue their talents, take note of their challenges and their progress, and remember them as stories. Recall these stories in times of difficulty to remind kids what they had to go through, how far they've come, and who they are.
- As you create stories, keep these ideas in mind:
  - Make the stories relevant to who kids are and want to be.
  - Use concrete details.
  - Create stories that make you feel as well think (that evoke emotions as well as thoughts).
  - Make stories that are easy to tell and easy to remember.

Let Kids Play

- Encourage kids to play early and often.
- Give kids time to mess around in the domain they are pursuing. For example, if they are musicians, let them goof off and get creative with their instruments sometimes, rather than relentlessly practicing all the time.
- Reward kids for simply going out and doing what they love.

Build Safety

- When you give feedback, send a clear message that you value the child.
- Listen intently.
- When you make a mistake, admit it.
- Make sure everyone has a voice.
- Embrace fun.

Allow and Show Vulnerability

- Be vulnerable yourself to signal that others can also be vulnerable. This builds trust and drives cooperation.
- Listen closely to hear a child's message, think, then respond.

Clarify Purpose

- Discuss with kids often why they are doing what they are doing—especially when they are struggling.
- Remind kids of their vocabulary, mantras, and stories.
- Help kids set process goals—for the short term and the long term—that focus on improving and learning.

CONCLUSION: ENJOY THE JOURNEY

Some kids have innate ability in certain areas: whether they can run a five-second forty-yard dash, or solve complex equations in a matter of seconds, or play and write music like nobody's business. These kids have a different starting place than other kids for developing their talent—if they choose to do so.

But innate ability isn't the only ingredient needed to realize talent. Talent needs to be developed. Talent is a journey, not a destination, and the starting place is just one spot on that journey.

That's true for everyone—but when it comes to kids, we adults don't always act like it's true. All too often, we tend to identify a kid as "talented" or not early in life, put them on a corresponding path, and call it done. While some kids may not reach the heights of achievement in the domains they pursue, it isn't our job to determine where their ceiling is—or that a ceiling even exists. Do we really want to stop a child's talent development by inventing an endpoint?

Every child deserves an opportunity to explore their talent before some adult says no. Kids too often do not get a choice in this matter—whether they are deemed "talented" and given all the opportunities that word affords, or deemed "untalented" and offered little or no opportunity. I don't advocate for coddling kids or shielding them from failure. Rather, I believe we should let kids try and let them fail and let them take a good hard look at their efforts and their progress—all while walking beside them on their journey, giving them a hand when they fall, and helping them figure out for themselves what to do next.

There is plenty of science in this book, and it's an essential component to understanding how talent development works and the role each of us adults can play in it. In my view, however, science is not the whole picture. I believe building talent is *also* an art. I encourage you to open your mind to the possibilities that lie within all kids—not just a few kids—as they pursue their talent, and use the science to support your art. Use the research, theories, real-life examples, and models in this book to help you create Talent Development Zones with and for kids. Most importantly, use your common sense and your passion for supporting a kid in who they want to be.

Remember our definition of talent: It is innate ability that can be improved. The talent that kids bear needs to be guided and assisted as it develops over time. In other words, it is a process. ***The pursuit of talent is talent itself.*** *Talent is what EVERY child bears and carries and brings forth over time.*

Enjoy the journey.

REFERENCES

Bailey, Richard, and David Collins. 2013. "The Standard Model of Talent Development and Its Discontents." *Kinesiology Review* 2 (4): 248–259. doi.org/10.1123/krj.2.4.248.

Bandura, Albert. 1994. "Self-Efficacy." In V. S. Ramachaudran, ed., *Encyclopedia of Human Behavior* 4: 71–81. New York: Academic Press. uky.edu/~eushe2/Bandura/BanEncy.html.

———. 2011. "On the Functional Properties of Perceived Self-Efficacy Revisited." *Journal of Management* 38 (1): 9–44. doi.org/10.1177/0149206311410606.

Bisanz, Jeffrey, Frederick J. Morrison, and Maria Dunn. 1995. "Effects of Age and Schooling on the Acquisition of Elementary Quantitative Skills." *Developmental Psychology* 31 (2): 221–236. doi.org/10.1037/0012-1649.31.2.221.

Blakemore, Sarah-Jayne. 2018. *Inventing Ourselves: The Secret Life of the Teenage Brain.* New York: Hachette.

Bodrova, Elena, and Deborah J. Leong. 2015. "Vygotskian and Post-Vygotskian Views on Children's Play." *American Journal of Play* 7 (3): 371–388. files.eric.ed.gov/fulltext/EJ1070266.pdf.

Burnett, Paul. 1999. "Children's Self-Talk and Academic Self-Concepts." *Educational Psychology in Practice* 15 (3): 195–200. doi.org/10.1080/0266736990150308.

Byer, Tom. 2016. *Football Starts at Home.* Tokyo: T3 International Ltd.

Calvin, Michael. 2017. *No Hunger in Paradise.* London: Cornerstone Penguin.

Chopra, Kamal. 2012. "Impact of Positive Self-Talk." *University of Lethbridge Faculty of Education.* opus.uleth.ca/bitstream/handle/10133/3202/Kamal%20Chopra.pdf.

Churchill, Winston. 1941. "Never Give In, Never, Never, Never, 1941." *America's National Churchill Museum.* nationalchurchillmuseum.org/never-give-in-never-never-never.html.

Cobley, Stephen, Jim McKenna, Joeseph Baker, and Nick Wattie. 2009. "How Pervasive Are Relative Age Effects in Secondary Education?" *Journal of Educational Psychology* 10 (2): 520–528. doi.org/10.1037/a0013845.

Collins, Dave, and Áine MacNamara. 2018. *Talent Development: A Practitioner Guide.* New York: Routledge.

Conversano, Ciro, Allesandro Rotondo, Elena Lensi, Olivia Della Vista, Prancesca Arpone, and Mario Antonio Reda. 2010. "Optimism and Its Impact on Mental and Physical Well-Being." *Clinical Practice and Epidemiology in Mental Health* 6: 25–29. doi.org/10.2174/1745017901006010025.

Coyle, Daniel. 2009. *The Talent Code: Greatness Isn't Born. It's Grown. Here's How.* New York: Bantam Dell.

———. 2018a. *The Culture Code: The Secrets of Highly Successful Groups.* New York: Bantam Books.

———. 2018b. "How Showing Vulnerability Helps Build a Stronger Team." TED, February 20, 2018. ideas.ted.com/how-showing-vulnerability-helps-build-a-stronger-team.

———. n.d. "Question and Answer." *Daniel Coyle.* Accessed September 15, 2021. danielcoyle.com/question-and-answer.

Creative Education Foundation. 2014. "Creative Problem Solving Resource Guide." creativeeducationfoundation.org/wp-content/uploads/2015/06/CPS-Guide-6-3-web.pdf.

Cuddy, Amy. 2015. *Presence: Bringing Your Boldest Self to Your Biggest Challenges.* New York: Back Bay Books.

Dev, Poonam C. 1996. "Intrinsic Motivation and the Student with Learning Disabilities." *Information Analyses* (070). files.eric.ed.gov/fulltext/ED403723.pdf.

———. 1997. "Intrinsic Motivation and Academic Achievement: What Does Their Relationship Imply for the Classroom Teacher?" *Remedial and Special Education* 18 (1): 12–19. doi.org/10.1177/074193259701800104.

Dreilinger, Danielle. 2019. "Up to 3.6 Million Students Should Be Labeled Gifted, but Aren't." *Hechinger Report,* November 26, 2019. hechingerreport.org/up-to-3-6-million-students-should-be-labeled-gifted-but-arent.

Duckworth, Angela. 2016. *Grit: The Power of Passion and Perseverance.* New York: Scribner.

———. n.d. "FAQ." *Angela Duckworth.* Accessed September 15, 2021. angeladuckworth.com/qa.

Duncker, Karl. 1945. "On Problem-Solving." *Psychological Monographs* 58 (5): i–113. doi.org/10.1037/h0093599.

Duval, Shelley, and Robert A. Wicklund. 1972. *A Theory of Objective Self-Awareness.* New York: Academic Press.

Dweck, Carol. 2015. "Carol Dweck Revisits the 'Growth Mindset.'" *Education Week,* September 22, 2015. edweek.org/leadership/opinion-carol-dweck-revisits-the-growth-mindset/2015/09.

———. 2016. *Mindset: The New Psychology of Success.* New York: Random House.

Dyer, Frank Lewis, and Thomas Commerford Martin. 1910. *Edison: His Life and Inventions.* New York: Harper and Brothers. gutenberg.org/files/820/820-h/820-h.htm.

Edmondson, Amy. 1999. "Psychological Safety and Learning Behavior in Work Teams." *Administrative Science Quarterly* 44 (2): 350–383. doi.org/10.2307/2666999.

Epstein, David. 2019. *Range: Why Generalists Triumph in a Specialized World.* New York: Riverhead Books.

Ericsson, K. Anders, Ralf Th. Krampe, and Clemens Tesch-Romer. 1993. "The Role of Deliberate Practice in the Acquisition of Expert Performance." *Psychological Review* 100 (3): 363–406. doi.org/10.1037/0033-295X.100.3.363.

Ericsson, Anders, and Robert Pool. 2016. *Peak: Secrets from the New Science of Expertise*. Boston: Houghton Mifflin Harcourt.

Eskreis-Winkler, Lauren. 2021. "Why Students Don't Learn from Failure." *Education Week,* June 1, 2021. edweek.org/teaching-learning/opinion-why-students-dont-learn-from-failure/2021/06.

Fenton, Sally A. M., Joan L. Duda, and Timothy Barrett. 2016. "Optimising Physical Activity Engagement During Youth Sport: A Self-Determination Theory Approach." *Journal of Sports Sciences* 34 (19): 1874–1884. doi.org/10.1080/02640414.2016.1142104.

Froman, Terry, and Aleksandr Shneydermann. 2013. "Relative Age Effect." Miami-Dade County Public Schools Research Brief 1205. drs.dadeschools.net/ResearchBriefs/RB1205.pdf.

Gagné, Françoys. 1985. "Giftedness and Talent: Reexamining a Reexamination of the Definitions." *Gifted Child Quarterly* 29 (3): 103–112. doi.org/10.1177/001698628502900302.

———. 1999. "Gagné's Differentiated Model of Giftedness and Talent." *Journal for the Education of the Gifted* 22 (2): 230–234. doi.org/10.1177/016235329902200209.

Gallardo-Gallardo, Eva, Nicky Dries, and Tomás F. González-Cruz. 2013. "What Is the Meaning of 'Talent' in the World of Work?" *Human Resources Management Review* 23 (4): 290–300. doi.org/10.1016/j.hrmr.2013.05.002.

Ghose, Tia. 2013. "Realistic Optimists May Have More Success and Happiness, Study Suggests." *Huffpost,* August 24, 2018. huffpost.com/entry/realistic-optimists_n_3816827.

Gladwell, Malcolm. 2002. *The Tipping Point: How Little Things Can Make a Big Difference*. Boston: Back Bay Books.

———. 2008. *Outliers: The Story of Success*. New York: Little, Brown.

Glass Ceiling Commission. 1995. "Good for Business: Making Full Use of the Nation's Human Capital." US Department of Labor. ecommons.cornell.edu/bitstream/handle/1813/79348/GlassCeiling FactFindingEnvironmentalScan.pdf.

Glucksberg, Sam, and Robert W. Weisberg. 1966. "Verbal Behavior and Problem Solving: Some Effects of Labeling in a Functional Fixedness Problem." *Journal of Experimental Psychology* 71 (5): 659–664. doi.org/10.1037/h0023118.

Godin, Seth. 2007. *The Dip: A Little Book That Teaches You When to Quit (and When to Stick)*. New York: Penguin.

Google. n.d. "Guide: Understand Team Effectiveness." *re:Work*. Accessed September 15, 2021. rework.withgoogle.com/guides/understanding-team-effectiveness/steps/introduction.

Gottfried, Adele Eskeles, Fleming, James S., and Gottfried, Allen W. 1994. "Role of Parental Motivational Practices in Children's Academic Intrinsic Motivation and Achievement." *Journal of Educational Psychology 86* (1): 104–113. doi.org/10.1037/0022-0663.86.1.104.

Guardian Sport. 2016. "'You Play Football with Your Head, and Your Legs Are There to Help You': Johan Cruyff in Quotes." *The Guardian*, March 24, 2016. theguardian.com/football/2016/mar/24/you-play-football-with-your-head-and-your-legs-are-there-to-help-you-johan-cruyff-in-quotes.

Hart, Susan, Annabelle Dixon, Mary Jane Drummond, and Donald McIntyre. 2004. *Learning Without Limits.* New York: Open University Press.

Harwood, Chris, Christopher Mark Spray, and Richard J. Keegan. 2008. "Achievement Goal Theories in Sport." In Thelma S. Horn (ed.). *Advances in Sport Psychology*, 157–185, 444–448. Champaign, IL: Human Kinetics.

Hattie, John, and Helen Timperley. 2007. "The Power of Feedback." *Review of Educational Research* 77 (1): 81–112. doi.org/10.3102/003465430298487.

Hattie, John A. C., and Gregory C. R. Yates. 2014. "Using Feedback to Promote Learning." In Victor A. Benassi, Catherine E. Overson, and Christopher M. Hakala (eds.), *Applying Science of Learning in Education: Infusing Psychological Science into the Curriculum*, teachpsych.org/ebooks/asle2014/index.php.

Isaacson, Walter. 2007. "20 Things You Need to Know About Albert Einstein." *Time,* April 5, 2007. content.time.com/time/specials/packages/article/0,28804,1936731_1936743_1936745,00.html.

Isaksen, Scott G., and Donald J. Treffinger. 2004. "Celebrating 50 Years of Reflective Practice: Versions of Creative Problem Solving." *Journal of Creative Behavior* 38 (2): 75–101. doi.org/10.1002/j.2162-6057.2004.tb01234.x.

Jiménez, Idafe Pérez, and Matthew T. G. Paine. 2008. "Relative Age Effect in Spanish Association Football: Its Extent and Implications for Wasted Potential." *Journal of Sports Sciences* 28 (10): 995–1003. doi.org/10.1080/02640410801910285.

Johnson, Eric. 2018. "Your Company's Culture Is Not Unique, Psychologist Adam Grant Says." *Vox,* June 30, 2018. vox.com/2018/6/30/17519694/adam-grant-psychology-management-culture-fit-kara-swisher-recode-decode-podcast.

Johnson, Wendy. 2013. "Excellence as a Manifestation of Experience-Producing Drives." In Scott Barry Kaufman, ed. *The Complexity of Greatness: Beyond Talent or Practice*, 3–16. New York: Oxford University Press.

Kannangara, Chathurika S., Rosie E. Allen, Gill Waugh, Nurun Nahar, Samia Zahraa, Noor Khan, Suzanne Rogerson, and Jerome Carson. 2018. "All That Glitters Is Not Grit: Three Studies of Grit in University Students." *Frontiers in Psychology* 9: 1539. doi.org/10.3389/fpsyg.2018.01539.

Keel, Toby. 2016. "Johan Cruyff's Best Quotes: The Game-Changing Wisdom of a True Football Legend." *Eurosport*, March 24, 2016. eurosport.com/football/johan-cruyff-s-best-quotes-the-game-changing-wisdom-of-a-true-football-legend_sto5366190/story.shtml.

Kerr, James. 2013. *Legacy: What the All Blacks Can Teach Us About the Business of Life*. London: Constable.

Korgaokar, Ajit, Dana K. Fuller, Richard S. Farley, and Jennifer L. Caputo. 2018. "Relative Age Effect Among Elite Youth Female Soccer Players across the United States." *SportMont* 16 (3): 37–41. doi.org/10.26773/smj.181007.

Library of Congress. n.d. "Life of Thomas Alva Edison." *Library of Congress*. Accessed September 15, 2021. loc.gov/collections/edison-company-motion-pictures-and-sound-recordings/articles-and-essays/biography/life-of-thomas-alva-edison.

Lucas, Suzanne. 2019. "How to Provide Constructive Feedback to Develop Employee Skills." *The Balance Careers*, September 3, 2019. thebalancecareers.com/constructive-feedback-to-help-employees-grow-4120943.

Luscombe, Belinda. 2018. "The Divorce Rate Is Dropping. That May Not Actually Be Good News." *Time*, November 26, 2018. time.com/5434949/divorce-rate-children-marriage-benefits.

Martin, Roy P., Patricia Foels, Greg Clanton, and Kathryn Moon. 2004. "Season of Birth Is Related to Child Retention Rates, Achievement, and Rate of Diagnosis of Specific LD." *Journal of Learning* 37 (4): 307–317. doi.org/10.1177/00222194040370040301.

McCarthy, Neil, and Dave Collins. 2014. "Initial Identification and Selection Bias Versus the Eventual Confirmation of Talent: Evidence for the Benefits of a Rocky Road?" *Journal of Sports Sciences* 32 (17) 1604–1610. doi.org/10.1080/02640414.2014.908322.

Montag, Ali. 2017. "The One Question You Should Always Ask in a Job Interview, According to Wharton's Top Professor." *CNBC*, July 24, 2017. cnbc.com/2017/07/24/adam-grant-the-1-question-you-should-always-ask-at-a-job-interview.html.

Moore, Lucinda. 2003. "Growing Up Maya Angelou." *Smithsonian Magazine*, April 2003. smithsonianmag.com/arts-culture/growing-up-maya-angelou-79582387.

Morrison, Frederick J., Lisa Smith, and Maureen Dow-Ehrensberger. 1995. "Education and Cognitive Development: A Natural Experiment." *Developmental Psychology* 31 (5): 789–799. doi.org/10.1037/0012-1649.31.5.789.

Moses, Toby. 2018. "Why Harry Kane Is an Inspiration to Chubby Children Everywhere." *The Guardian*, July 9, 2018. theguardian.com/football/shortcuts/2018/jul/09/harry-kane-inspiration-chubby-children-everywhere.

Musch, Jochin, and Simon Grondin. 2001. "Unequal Competition as an Impediment to Personal Development: A Review of the Relative Age Effect in Sport." *Developmental Review* 21 (2): 147–167. doi.org/10.1006/drev.2000.0516.

National Association for Gifted Children. 2021a. "Identification." *National Association for Gifted Children*. Accessed September 15, 2021. nagc.org/resources-publications/gifted-education-practices/identification.

— —. 2021b. "What Is Giftedness?" *National Association for Gifted Children.* Accessed September 15, 2021. nagc.org/resources-publications/resources/what-giftedness.

Newsweek Special Edition. 2015. "Michael Jordan Didn't Make Varsity—At First." *Newsweek,* October 17, 2015. newsweek.com/missing-cut-382954.

New Zealand Rugby. n.d. "Match Centre." *All Blacks.* Accessed September 15, 2021. stats.allblacks.com.

O'Connor, Thomas Power, ed. 1907. "The Wizard of Electricity." *T. P.'s Weekly* 10 (November 29): 695. babel.hathitrust.org/cgi/pt?id=coo.31924069714339&view=1up&seq=699.

Osborn, Alex F. 1953. *Applied Imagination: Principles and Procedures of Creative Thinking.* New York: Charles Scribner's Sons.

Pink, Dan. 2009. "The Puzzle of Motivation." *TED,* July 2009. ted.com/talks/dan_pink_the_puzzle_of _motivation /transcript.

Rasmussen, Heather N., Michael F. Scheier, and Joel B. Greenhouse. 2010. "Optimism and Physical Health: A Meta-analytic Review." *Annals of Behavioral Medicine* 37 (3): 239–256. doi.org/10.1007/s12160-009-9111-x.

Ravizza, Ken. 1998. *Heads-Up Baseball: Playing the Game One Pitch at a Time. Chicago: Masters Press.*

Redmond, Brian Francis. 2016. "Psych 484: Work Attitudes and Job Motivation: 7. Self-Efficacy and Social Cognitive Theories." *Penn State University Wikispaces.* wikispaces.psu.edu/display/PSYCH484/7.+Self-Efficacy +and+Social+Cognitive+Theories.

Reilly, Katie. 2017. "'I Wish You Bad Luck. Read Supreme Court Justice John Roberts' Unconventional Speech to His Son's Graduating Class." *Time,* July 5, 2017. time.com/4845150/chief-justice -john-roberts -commencement-speech-transcript.

Ritchotte, Jennifer, Chin-Wen Lee, and Amy Graefe. 2020. *Start Seeing and Serving Underserved Gifted Students: 50 Strategies for Equity and Excellence.* Minneapolis: Free Spirit Publishing.

Rosenthal, Robert, and Lenore Jacobson. 1968. "Pygmalion in the Classroom." *The Urban Review* 3 (1): 16–20. doi.org/10.1007/BF02322211.

Rosoff, Matt. 2016. "The Only Reason the Mac Looks Like It Does Is Because Steve Jobs Dropped in on a Course Taught by This Former Monk." *Business Insider,* March 8, 2016. businessinsider.com/robert-palladino -calligraphy-class-inspired-steve-jobs-2016-3.

Segev, Elad, and Sorel Cahan. 2014. "Older Students Have a Greater Chance to Be Accepted to Gifted Student Programmes." *Assessment in Education: Principles, Policy & Practice* 21 (1): 4–15. doi.org/10.1080/09695 94X.2013.822847.

Shaw, Quincy. 2016. *Edison.* Boston: New Word City.

Shute, Valerie J. 2008. "Focus on Formative Feedback." *Review of Educational Research* 78 (1): 153–189. doi.org/10.3102/0034654307313795.

Sproull, Patrick. 2014. "I Never Hypnotised My Principal! That Part I Made Up." *The Guardian*, November 24, 2014. theguardian.com/childrens-books-site/2014/nov/24/dav-pilkey-captain-underpants-interview.

Street, Elizabeth. 2017. "The Moving Story of How a Teacher Inspired Maya Angelou to Speak." *Learning Liftoff*, May 8, 2017. learningliftoff.com/how-a-teacher-inspired-maya-angelou-to-speak.

Swann, Mandy, Alison Peacock, Susan Hart, and Mary Jane Drummond. 2012. *Creating Learning Without Limits*. New York: Open University Press.

Thomas, Mark. n.d. "7 Lessons for the Corporate World from the Greatest Team in the World." *PPI Network*. Accessed September 15. 2021. theppinetwork.com/media/articles/7-lessons-corporate-world -greatest-team-world.

TOVO Institute. n.d. "A Modern Methodology." Accessed September 15, 2021. tovoinstitute.com/methodology.

US Department of Education. 1965. "Elementary and Secondary Education Act of 1965." ed.gov/documents /essa-act-of-1965.pdf.

———. 2004. "Title IX—General Provisions." 20 U.S.C. 7801. ed.gov/policy/elsec/leg/esea02/pg107.html.

Wharton School. 2016. "Beyond 10,000 Hours of Practice: What Experts Do Differently." *Knowledge@Wharton*, May 19. 2016. knowledge.wharton.upenn.edu/article/anders-ericsson-book-interview-peak-secrets-from.

Wilson, Gabriel. 2006. "The Effects of External Rewards on Intrinsic Motivation." studylib.net/doc/8907712 /the-effects-of-external-rewards-on-intrinsic-motivation.

Woods, Julie. 2016. "State and Federal Policy: Gifted and Talented Youth." *Education Commission of the States*. ecs.org/wp-content/uploads/State_and_Federal_Policy_for_Gifted_and_Talented_Youth.pdf.

Yerkes, Robert M., and John D. Dodson. 1908. "The Relation of Strength of Stimulus to Rapidity of Habit-Formation." *Journal of Comparative Neurology and Psychology* 18 (5): 459–482. doi.org/10.1002 /cne.920180503.

Zirkel, Sabrina. 2002. "Is There a Place for Me? Role Models and Academic Identity Among White Students and Students of Color." *Teachers College Record* 104 (2): 357–376. doi.org/10.1111/1467-9620.00166.

INDEX

ABOUT THE AUTHOR

Dr. Lee Hancock is a professor, performance psychology coach, and program creator who works with students, athletes, coaches, educators, parents, organizations, and other high-level performers. Lee earned his Master's and Ph.D. from Arizona State University and is a tenured professor of kinesiology at California State University Dominguez Hills. He has had a private practice for more than twenty years, where he has worked with athletes from youth to professional and with classroom teachers, students, and parents of awesome kids. Dr. Hancock is also an internationally recognized speaker and author. Most importantly, he is a dad of three high-energy, competitive, caring boys. Each time he engages with a person or a group, his goal is always the same: to help them be more prepared to perform their best—when it counts! He lives in Los Angeles, California.

Other Great Resources from Free Spirit

Bright, Complex Kids
Supporting Their Social and Emotional Development
by Jean Sunde Peterson, Ph.D., and Daniel B. Peters, Ph.D.
Grades K–12.
152 pp.; PB; 7¼" x 9¼".
Free PLC / Book Study Guide
freespirit.com / PLC

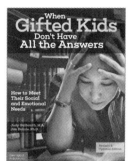

When Gifted Kids Don't Have All the Answers
How to Meet Their Social and Emotional Needs
(Revised & Updated Edition)
by Judy Galbraith, M.A., and Jim Delisle, Ph.D.
For teachers, gifted coordinators, guidance counselors, and parents of gifted children grades K–9.
288 pp.; PB; B&W photos; 7¼" x 9¼"; includes digital content.

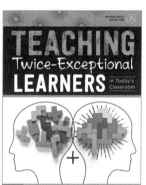

Teaching Twice-Exceptional Learners in Today's Classroom
by Emily Kircher-Morris, M.A., M.Ed., LPC
Grades K–12.
248 pp.; PB; 8½" x 11"; includes digital content.
Free PLC / Book Study Guide
freespirit.com / PLC

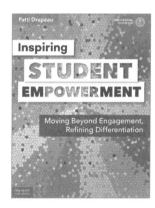

Inspiring Student Empowerment
Moving Beyond Engagement, Refining Differentiation
by Patti Drapeau
For educators, grades K–12.
208 pp.; PB; 8½" x 11"; includes digital content.
Free PLC / Book Study Guide
freespirit.com / PLC

Start Seeing and Serving Underserved Gifted Students
50 Strategies for Equity and Excellence
by Jennifer Ritchotte, Ph.D., Chin-Wen Lee, Ph.D., and Amy Graefe, Ph.D.
For educators and administrators of grades K–8.
192 pp.; PB; 8½" x 11"; includes digital content.
Free PLC / Book Study Guide
freespirit.com / PLC

Empowering Underrepresented Gifted Students
Perspectives from the Field
edited by Joy Lawson Davis, Ed.D., and Deb Douglas, M.S.
Grades K–12.
208 pp.; PB; 8½" x 11".

Smarts! Everybody's Got Them

by Thomas Armstrong, Ph.D., illustrated by Tim Palin

For ages 5–9.

44 pp.; HC; full-color; 11¼" x 9¼".

Mindset Power

A Kid's Guide to Growing Better Every Day

by Shannon Anderson, illustrated by Violet Lemay

For ages 9–13.

128 pp.; PB; 2-color; 6" x 9".

You're Smarter Than You Think

A Kid's Guide to Multiple Intelligences (Revised & Updated Edition)

by Thomas Armstrong, Ph.D.

For ages 9–14.

208 pp.; PB; 2-color; illust.; 7" x 9".

What Do You Really Want?

How to Set a Goal and Go for It! A Guide for Teens (Revised & Updated Edition)

by Beverly K. Bachel

For ages 11 & up.

160 pp.; PB; 2- color; 6" x 9".

Y Is for Yet

A Growth Mindset Alphabet

by Shannon Anderson, illustrated by Jacob Souva

For ages 4–8.

40 pp.; HC; full-color; 8¼" x 9".

Dream Up Now™

The Teen Journal for Creative Self-Discovery

by Rayne Lacko, with community outreach advisor Lesley Holmes

For ages 13 & up.

176 pp.; PB with layflat binding; 1-color; 7¼" x 9¼".

Interested in purchasing multiple quantities and receiving volume discounts?
Contact edsales@freespirit.com or call 1.800.735.7323 and ask for Education Sales.

Many Free Spirit authors are available for speaking engagements, workshops, and keynotes.
Contact speakers@freespirit.com or call 1.800.735.7323.

For pricing information, to place an order, or to request a free catalog, contact:

Free Spirit Publishing Inc.
6325 Sandburg Road, Suite 100
Minneapolis, MN 55427-3674

toll-free 800.735.7323 • local 612.338.2068
fax 612.337.5050 • help4kids@freespirit.com • freespirit.com